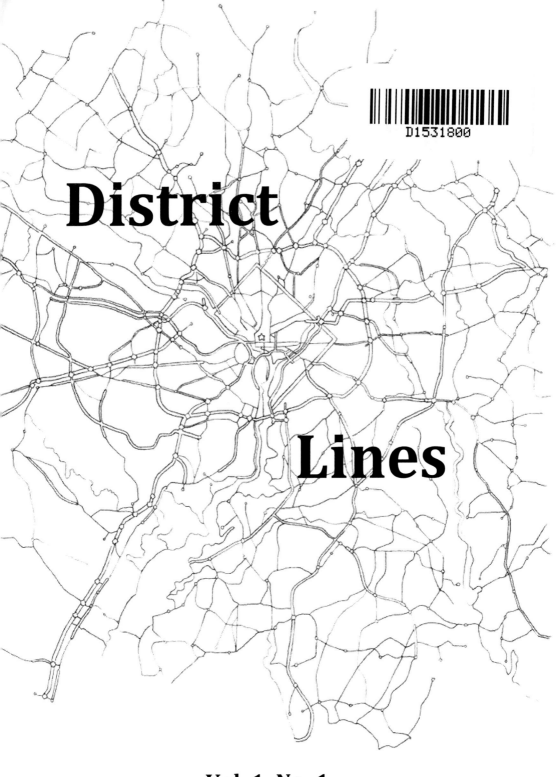

District

Lines

Vol. 1, No. 1
Summer 2013

D1531800

Published by Politics & Prose Bookstore
5015 Connecticut Avenue NW
Washington, D.C. 20008, U.S.A.

Phone: (202) 364-1919

Email: books@politics-prose.com

Website: www.politics-prose.com

ISBN: 978-1-62429-009-1

2

This book was printed on Opus, the Espresso Book Machine located in the fiction room at Politics & Prose Bookstore. To learn more about printing your manuscript on Opus, visit us online at www.politics-prose.com/opus. To get started printing with Opus, email opus@politics-prose.com or call (202) 349-1182.

Politics & Prose Bookstore

Founded in 1984, Politics & Prose Bookstore is Washington, D.C.'s premier independent bookstore and cultural hub, a gathering place for people interested in reading and discussing books. Politics & Prose offers superior service, a wide range of book choices, and a haven for book lovers.

District Lines

Editorial Staff
Emma Bushnell
Susan Coll
Bill Leggett
Rose Levine
Mark Moran
Hannah Oliver
Michael Ravenscroft

Cover Art and Icons
Art Hondros

Maps and P&P Store Drawings
Frans Boukas

Help Along the Way
Sarah Baline
Dana Chidiac
Alexandra Donahue
Carrie Dulaney
Lacey Dunham
David Maritz
Jeanie Teare
Lars Townsend
Angela Williams

In a city like Washington, known for its lobbyists and lawyers, its academics and politicians, it's easy to overlook the thriving arts scene in and around the District of Columbia. At Politics & Prose, we're keenly aware of the unique artistic character of our community. So we decided to establish our own forum for local artists, both published and previously unpublished, known and unknown, to share their reflections on the neighborhoods in which they live. With the blessing of the store's new owners, Bradley Graham and Lissa Muscatine, *District Lines* was born.

It took us nearly a year to organize this project, with P&P staff members contributing time largely on a volunteer basis. At first we weren't sure whether any writers would be interested in submitting pieces. After all, another literary magazine? An old school, paper-and-glue affair in a digital age? Our skepticism was answered in the most heartwarming way when our call for submissions generated well over 100 responses.

Although we weren't able to publish everything, we're excited about bringing such a wide range of experience and perspective together in a single anthology. In this collection, you'll find poetry, essays, short fiction, sketches, and photography about subjects as quirky as a whispering exit on the Capitol Beltway, a sighting of Effi Barry on a Metro bus, an August night on the Q Street Bridge, hotcakes at the Florida Avenue Grill, and an ode to the Dupont Circle metro escalator. And a particular favorite of ours: an account by the wife of a plumber who worked at the White House from Truman to Carter.

We welcome your feedback on *District Lines,* Volume 1, Issue 1. Keep an eye out for Issue 2!

– Susan Coll

Contents

REMEMBRANCE

TRANSIENCE

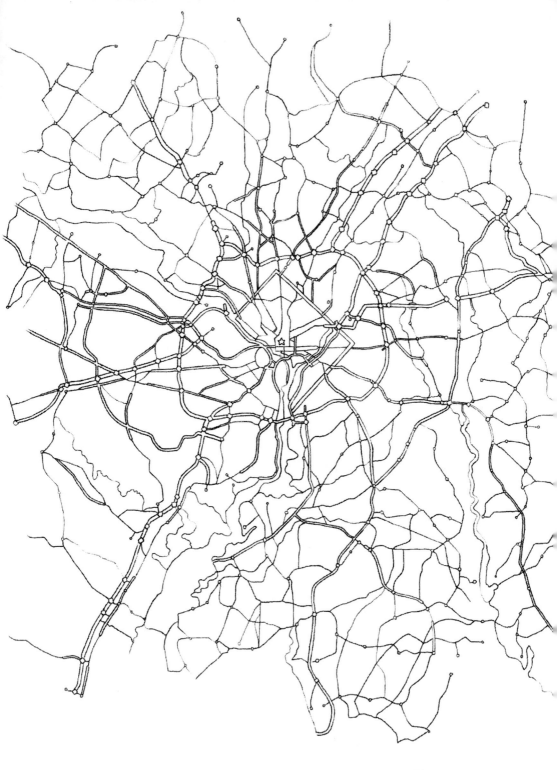

Atmospheres.

ON THE C&O CANAL
by Linda Pastan

When we walk together, you
with your crest of silvery curls,
a bright scarf at your neck,

me in my faded jacket,
2 buttons missing, my hair
an ordinary shade of brown,

we're like those mallards
we stop to watch: the male,
his head an iridescent

green—the color of jade,
or emerald stones polished
by water,

the female in her dowdy
coat—straight off the rack—
of dullest feathers.

And yet how peaceful,
even regal they seem,
paddling along,

dragging a shimmering wake
(like all our years together)
behind them.

Linda Pastan *has published thirteen books, most recently* Traveling Light. *She is a past Poet Laureate of Maryland and in 2003 won the Ruth Lily Prize for lifetime achievement.*

BEHIND THE COUNTER AT THE FLORIDA AVENUE GRILL

by Karla Daly

People have to eat, so my job is safe.
Omelets all day,
hotcakes like a plate full of halos,
meatloaf with a pillow of candied yams.
Tastes so good, you might think you're in love with me
and bring me roses.
It's just the biscuits and gravy talking.
See you next week, I say as you leave,
because I will.

On the outside, I am starched, pressed, and hair-netted.
I am pepper, sugar, salt, three feet of spotless counter, pepper, sugar, salt.
I am neatly stacked coffee mugs and cereal bowls.
I am stainless-steel tiles that gleam but don't reflect
the hungry souls who face me.

But I am hungry, too.

On the inside, I am half-smoked with ideas, orange-juiced with ambition,
and scrappled with frustration.
I am that sticky, half-used bottle of syrup.
I am the week-old roses in a vase on the counter
ready to cry petals into a bowl of grits.

So forgive me if I duck behind the counter
and write on the back of an order.
Have to dream when I can.

How else will French toast become sonnets
and scrambled eggs, free verse?

Karla Daly is a freelance writer and editor living in Washington, DC. Her poetry recently appeared in The Prose-Poem Project. "Behind the Counter at the Florida Avenue Grill" was inspired by a photo by Christine Pearl.

ZAMBONI (for the Washington Capitals)
by Fonda Bell Miller

this is ice hockey
skates siss
sticks clatter
bodies slam
slap of the puck
the players
gladiators
glide
collide
fight to the rim of life

there will be a win and a loss
but now the drone of the Zamboni
with its slow shaving rinsing
swishing over the surface
of the ice continues until the ice
is smooth flat silken
a glacier in moonlight

the driver of the Zamboni
who wants perhaps to be
the player
the gladiator
prepares again
the surface of the world
for a continuing game
a different battle
a new and somehow perfect
little war without death

Fonda Bell Miller *lives in Alexandria, VA. Her poems have appeared in* Little Patuxent Review, Poet Lore, The CS Monitor, Light Quarterly, Frogpond *and other places. She enjoys watching the Caps play and also watching the Zamboni.*

Sketch 1 – Farmer's Market

Marguerite Beck-Rex *is a lifelong writer and more recent artist. Her sketchbook and pen are with her always. Marguerite exhibits frequently, has coordinated many artist trips to Provence, coordinates a biennial Van Ness North Cooperative art exhibit and is an active member of the Women's Caucus for Art, DC Chapter.*

SIRIUS RISING ON CONNECTICUT
by Juanita Adams

Heat index 105; temperature: a hundred two
Traffic's orchestra drones ceaselessly;
And beneath my urban 9th-floor window
Wailing trimmers compete
With cicada mating calls;
Limp figures glide in slow motion
And images distort like mirages;
On this swampy 8th-month day
I yield, wilt, and sleep

Juanita Adams *is a retired Public Affairs Officer of the U.S.
Department of State. Her lifetime interests have included the
performing and studio arts. She is a member of the Jackson Art
Center of Georgetown.*

OF A BROKEN-HEARTED RIVER
by Anna El-Eini

"Son, if you could see it now. Sunlight split into a thousand beams o' light. There'd be dancing diamonds all the way out over the water."

My Nana and I sit on her porch overlooking the river. The sun rests above the cottonwood and poplar trees sending long shadows shifting across the garden. The river slips by, muddy and slow. I close my eyes and try to picture sunlight dancing on clear, glassy water.

"Now look it. Sunlight falls down dead, got nowhere to go."

Nana still lives in the same house my great grandfather built over a hundred years ago. One of the few places people like us were allowed to live. She was baptized here, on the riverbank at the end of the garden path. She grew up running around the garden, helping her Daddy with his vegetable patch and swimming in the river every day she could. I tell you though, she's been left pretty much faithless by what's happened to this river in the past 50 years.

"It ain't never gonna be like that again. Sweet boy, maybe in your lifetime, but not in mine."

Nana's grown tired of hoping she'll ever see the water again the way she remembers it. Sometimes she takes her rocker into the house and reads inside because she can't bear to look out at what's become of her river. On a bad day, when she sees an old shopping cart or a tire dragged along by the river, she even turns the chair to face away from the window. I asked her once why she didn't move someplace else.

"I know we allowed to live other places now. But I also know they got us racked and stacked in buildings high up as the sky. No, son, I won't ever be movin'."

Since the water first changed color and all the light went out of it, she hasn't once walked down to the riverbank. In the 18 years I've been on this earth, we've never stood together by the water, my Nana and me. But I never knew the river any other way. I never knew it when it splintered sunlight and fell like cool raindrops all over the children who played in it. So I'm always wondering, what was it like then? I stand at the edge of the river sometimes, I watch the birds wading like delicate old ladies and flying around like they have important meetings to get to, and the old men fishing because they always have, and I think to myself, there's a heron trying to be a heron over there—are there really fish trying to be fish in that dark, dirty water too?

I'll tell you how it happened, how come this river all but died. People like my Nana remember how the munitions factory poisoned the water in just the few years it took to get ready for and finish the Second World War. And I've seen for myself how the land that's being cleared for development, faster than a rabbit can dig a hole, is washing into the river and making it narrow as a piece of string. I know there's sewage flows from the old treatment plant into the river every time it rains—that's partly how come my Nana won't go near it. But I also know it's the fault of regular people too. All that stuff we buy and the things we eat and the things we drink. I know because I've seen it all, strung along the riverbank like a cheap pawnshop necklace.

I came here tonight to tell Nana the news. I'm going to college in California next year, to study water. Full scholarship. If it weren't so far from Nana, I'd be the happiest kid on the planet right now. She just about raised me with my Mom and Dad working so hard my whole life.

"Why d'you have to go so far away? Thought your Mr. Lowe wanted you to go to North Carolina?"

This is true. My science teacher wanted me to apply to all the Carolina colleges.

"Son, they have just about a million, million hogs crapping into their rivers down there," he said. "You want to study water and how to clean it up, that's the place."

But I have my heart set on the West Coast. The college I'm going to is practically sitting on the beach. One day I'm going to take a road trip all the way up that coast, and any place I can, I'm going to get out and put my feet in the clear, blue ocean.

"You gonna forget us, son. I'm so scared we'll lose you."

I put my arm around her strong shoulders, and hold her tight. Her slender, dark face is lined and furrowed from living out her 60 years but her skin is still soft against mine. Her deep, hazel eyes gloss with tears that I know she'll cry only after I leave.

"No, Nana, never. I'm going so I can come back."

The Anacostia River has a way of making you come back. Even on days when you stand staring out at the dull water and shake your head at the trash curled up like a whole lot of unwanted stray cats along its banks, you just know you're going to be back here soon. That's what I've done my whole life, no matter that Nana always told me never to go near the water. When I got my first job, stocking shelves at the shabby little grocery store on my street corner, I saved so I could buy myself a pair of the big waders just like the ones you see on the fly fishing shows on TV. I've been going down to the river ever since to dig. I pull up trash and haul it into a big trash bag and when that one's full, I get to work on another one. Sometimes Nana lets me shower at her place afterwards and she fixes me a big dinner and tells me she's proud of me. Other times, she shakes her head, and says, no. Not today. It makes her too sad to see me muddy and tired, hauling trash that she knows came out of the river she was supposed to have found God in.

It's getting cold out on the porch and Nana and I reluctantly head inside to get ready for bed. With me leaving in a few weeks, every one of these evenings together is weighed and counted. Tomorrow's a big day for me, one of my favorite days of the year, and I have to get some rest. Clean-up Day. It's one of the days I don't feel so foolish and alone, when hundreds and hundreds of people come out and work all day to clean up this river. Every year I meet some nice people. Every year I leave feeling like we're never ever going to give up because this river, I tell you, it has a way of making you come back.

Here they come now, all the volunteers. I'm helping with sign-in and giving out T-shirts. There's a family of three in front of me. The girl is little; she can't be more than five.

"These are for you," I say, handing them each a T-shirt and a nametag.

The dad, Ian, holds up the lime green T-shirt and says, "It's a bit bright!"

"Good, you'll be easier to spot when you fall in," says the mom, Linda, laughing.

I like these guys, they're funny. The little girl is writing her name, *Sandra*, in cute, girly letters and she asks me for crayons so she can draw some butterflies and flowers around it.

"You guys are with me, and my girlfriend, Sheryl," I decide aloud.

When I'm done with sign-in, I round up my group of volunteers and we go down to the dock to take a boat to the clean-up site.

"So, three hours 'til high tide," I say. "Ready to get to work?"

"Three hours," Ian says slowly, yawning. Sandra yawns too and looks around sleepily. Her Mom hugs and nuzzles her. I wonder what made them come, this family? I know they live on the other side of town; I saw their address on the sign-in sheet. We get a lot of white volunteers, but they're usually from along the west side of the river—Capitol Hill, Eastern Market—not too far to come, and close enough to the river to care about it.

We wait a long time for a boat to arrive and when it does, I'm kind of embarrassed. It's a battered, shaky old thing. I'm not even sure we're allowed to take this many folk on it, because the motor runs pretty angry. But the good thing is, it wakes Sandra right up and now she's laughing with her Dad. As the boat grinds along, I watch the changing light of day wash across the sky. I sit back and look around at the few swallows and gulls that aren't traumatized by the violent noise of the engine, and I'm mesmerized by the turbulent waters behind us.

When we get to the clean-up site I hand out trash bags to the volunteers.

"So you guys know what you're doing?"

"Oh, yeah, we come here every year—don't ask me, *why*?" Ian says, laughing, but then his face goes funny. "Shoot! I'm sinking. I can't move."

Sheryl laughs, pointing to where Ian's feet are rapidly disappearing into the thick muck at the water's edge.

Sandra giggles. "Look at the mud coming out of my Daddy's shoes!"

"Should have worn bigger boots," I say, laughing too, because now the mud has kind of oozed half way up Ian's legs and it looks like he stepped in paint. I got to say, though, Ian looks miserable. And now that I stop to think about it, I don't blame him. If it was me, I'd be worrying too. I know this river's nothing but a toxic soup, and now he's got it all in his shoes. He's right to worry. I've seen the three-eyed fish and the tumors on all of them dead animals and birds the old fishermen in my Nana's neighborhood pull out just about every other day. I can't believe that man, Ian, though. He just pulls himself together and now he's gone up the bank, I guess to take his anger out on the trash. He gets right to work collecting the mountains of Styrofoam scraps, old pens, plastic bottles, diapers, tennis balls, and what looks like all the straws in the world, lying about everywhere. Linda's working hard on the grocery bags suffocating the scrappy little tree saplings, and Sandra gets hold of one end of a broken lampshade stuck in the thick mud. As I watch that little girl, I'm not too happy she's here. There's deadly bacteria, all kinds of chemicals, human waste and animal waste deep in this mud, and in the water itself. This much I know. Toxic soup, like I said. All the reasons why my Nana knows the damage done this river can't soon be undone. I work alongside Ian; I fill up my bags one after another, like I always do. He looks up suddenly and says, "Look at this place, Damien. What the hell happened?" And I swear I see tears in the man's eyes.

He wanders off to work alone and Sandra joins her mom, Sheryl and me as we walk to an area downstream that looks like a suitcase exploded all over it. Clothes are scattered everywhere, torn and shredded in pieces, caught on every twig and rock, embedded in the roots of the trees rising off the bank. There are tires that must have been lifted at high tide to the top of the embankment, a leaf blower, a hair dryer, thousands and thousands more straws, disposable pens and cigarette ends. I tell you, it is hard, backbreaking work to free all of this from the mud and gather it into the garbage bags.

Linda, Sheryl and I pull together on a stubborn tire, buried deep in the mud. We're all cursing and laughing loud and having difficulty putting our best effort into the job.

I call over to Sandra. "*Come on girl*—what are you standing around for? We need all the hands we can get to move this slimy ol' tire!"

As she steps forward bravely to join in, she slips and falls on her backside. She lands on something—a brown plastic horse—and wipes it off.

"Is it O.K. to keep this Mommy?"

Her Mom nods. It's probably the only thing of any interest that little girl has found all morning.

The rain's come and gone, and now look at us. We're all soaked, hot and muddy, waiting for our boat to rescue us. You should see what we have. Seventy or more full garbage bags, a bunch of tires, car batteries, three shopping carts, a fridge door, an old dryer drum, eight broken TVs, two laptops, a bag full of cell phones, all piled together. The tide's working its mischief and we don't have a whole lot of shore to stand on now. That little Sandra, the closer the water gets, the more excited she is about getting soaked by the river. She doesn't know what mercury does to soft tissues. Before anyone can stop her, she runs and soaks herself, splashing about and giggling happily.

"It's so *muddy*! But it's not cold. It's *warm!*" she shouts.

Ian and I are on her in a second, pulling her out as though she's getting ready to drown. I see horror in the eyes of the adults lined up along the shore. She must see it too because she says, laughing, "I'm O.K. I'm just wet!"

Oh, sweet girl, you sweet thing, you're *not* O.K. This river is not O.K. It's not a place to splash, glide and swim on a hot summer's day. As Ian and Linda fuss over their girl, I picture in my mind for the first time ever, my Nana as a little girl. She's playing in the river, just like Sandra—only the water is clear and pure. There she is, ducking and diving. I mourn for that child.

The boat is here at last but it can only take a few passengers, so Ian goes back with Sandra and Sheryl. Linda and I are getting ready to give up being rescued when another boat comes by, with a canoe tied behind it.

"Do we get in the boat or the canoe?" Linda asks.

The driver unties the canoe and pushes it toward us. "We've got two motors down and volunteers up and down the river to rescue. Count yourself lucky."

I don't feel very lucky. Linda and I are tired, wet and really filthy.

"Come on then, Damien," Linda says. "I guess it's this or we swim for it."

We've already shared all the life stories you can talk about with a stranger, so we shift to what's around us. She points out a red-tailed hawk flying overhead and a great blue heron feeding after the rain. I spot a raccoon and an osprey. The osprey just about breaks me up inside after the morning we've had. A creature that beautiful doesn't belong on a river like this. I lay my oar on my lap and trail my hand in the murky water, forgetting that I shouldn't. Linda's sitting up front of me. She moves the oar up and down, smooth and slow.

"Aren't you supposed to see through water?" she says. "See fish and rocks and grass? Don't you think sometimes, it's like the river is just trying to breathe?"

We turn together to look at the water and we drift silently with the tide. After a while, Linda lifts her arm up and points downstream.

"The river's widening up here. Is this where we turn?"

I tell her yes, but I can't help feeling as though the river has opened up to embrace us, begging our love.

I sit with Sheryl, waiting for my Nana to bring dinner out onto the porch. While we showered and changed, she made my favorite chicken and peas and she even baked a rhubarb and strawberry pie.

"How come we're eating out here tonight?"

"Wasn't just you today."

"So you're happy?"

"No son, not happy. Just a little touched, is all."

"Touched by what?"

"I saw them boats go by piled high as the heavens. Heard 'em first, they so loud. I saw what you all did today. You eat up. Both of you must be bone-tired and hungry."

It's hard to stay awake as we eat, and I fall happily into bed as soon as I drag myself upstairs. On the nightstand is the little toy horse Sandra found. She gave it to me when we said goodbye, and I've washed it and scrubbed it clean. That girl has been baptized in the Anacostia River and taken it into her heart. When I close my eyes, I see straws, cigarettes, Bic pens, Styrofoam, diapers, plastic grocery bags, shopping carts, tires, clothes and plastic bottles. I see all the trash of modern life that litters and chokes the banks and waters of the Anacostia River. But when I dream, I see diamonds dancing on the river and a little girl diving and rising up out of the water, her pigtails dripping clear drops of sunlight onto her smooth, black shoulders.

Anna El-Eini was born in Sudan and grew up in England before moving to the United States. She was a policy analyst and community organizer in Washington, DC before turning to writing full-time. She is currently working on two novels while finishing her first collection of short stories.

Q STREET BRIDGE
by Jody Bolz

Accept this stranded season in the city,
wet streets lamp-lit, distances unclear.

We'll stand on the bridge and watch the night
make forests of these parks. The dark

adapts us, slides to the horizon—and we're
tropical and prosperous in the August air.

Jody Bolz is the author of A Lesson in Narrative Time *(Gihon Books, 2004) and* Shadow Play *(forthcoming from Turning Point Books). Her poems have appeared in such journals as* The American Scholar, Indiana Review, North American Review, Ploughshares, *and* Poetry East--*and in many literary anthologies. She edits* Poet Lore, *established in 1889.*

IT SNOWED AS IN A FAIRY TALE
by Patric Pepper

It Snowed As In A Fairy Tale,

and we were giddy, knocking through the sideways
    slanting crazy-making snow,
fresh from the cautionary joy of WTOP radio,
as if we didn't know where we were walking— straight down
    Rhode Island Avenue NE
with the hiss and rattle of vehicles, the usual snafu
Washington becomes. We heard a whizzing Metro

pass above our heads, heard it whine to a stop. I
    looked up through the blow
of flakes at the very moment a very resolute freight train
    pushed past the growing traffic fiasco,
and then your boot kicked up a lump covered in white:
    a withered sparrow, oh!
                And still we were giddy.

Our boots: Our boots lumbered up Twelfth Street,
    left on Monroe.
We made the Shrine by two o'clock, that gigantic
    limestone curio,
authority in white one might easily misconstrue
but for the dinging of its bells inexplicably dinging then,
    as if the Shrine were dingy too.
Then Glenwood Cemetery—nearly home!—the stones
    with jaunty hats of snow in a soft white meadow,
             and we were giddy.

Patric Pepper *lives in Washington, DC. He is the author of a chapbook,* Zoned Industrial, *and a full length collection,* Temporary Apprehensions. *His work has most recently appeared in* Ekphrasis, Fugue, Gargoyle Magazine, Passager, *and* BAP Quarterly *(online). Since 2007 he has served as president of Washington Writers' Publishing House, a regional nonprofit writers' cooperative publishing poetry and fiction collections in the Baltimore and Washington area. He is editor and publisher of* Pond Road Press.

LADY FINGERS AND BONE CHINA
SMITHSONIAN CRAFTS FAIR, 1996
by Nancy Allinson

A ceramic nose on the lid of the teapot,
meant for lifting with two fingers.
A nose with nostrils like flat raisins
where no breath could possibly escape,
a nose that could break
if you dropped it—
not punchable though,
not a smeller of bad breath
or lies left on the table
after a morning of gossip and hot tea,
with women who want more than bone china,
who'd love a tea set with body parts
smooth and functional—
yielding results.
So they write out their checks
to the potter who sells mugs
with painted red lips near the rims
and fingers for handles.
The women crowd around;
they want more than the tea leaves
scattered
for someone else to read.

Nancy Allinson is a Maryland poet whose work has appeared in
Poet Lore, Minimus, Potomac Review, *and* Beltway Poetry
Quarterly. *She is also a winner of the "Bethesda 8" Trolley Poetry
Bench competition. She is a former D.C. resident and a recent
federal government retiree.*

AVENUES TO THE HILLTOP
by Andrea Adleman

Hills

This hill is gentler.

It is accessible to the pedestrian. It raises its voice only on the weariest of days, its elevation noted in the final taxing steps of the homeward march.

This hill is storied. Its trees shelter memories of craftsmen who imagined a nation and demarcated a capital with a capitol on the hill. This hill is confident, ascending with purpose and giving rise to monumental visions at once fantastic and concrete. This hill commands the crossroads, delineating quadrants across the grid bisected by the avenues that lure demagogues and dollars and dreamers and diplomats and developers to a district of the disenfranchised.

This hill is surmountable. An ambitious stride is sufficiently powerful to summit its slope. This hill does not spiral to disorienting heights along the rim of the world. It harbors no likeness to the sinuous pass between basin and valley where the sun sets and angels reign.

Upheaval

Seismic friction strikes this hill one summer day, rupturing the afternoon routine with otherworldly sensations. A restless impulse sparks momentary chaos. Structure succumbs to the unknown. History is dislodged.

This hill regains its ground. This hill does not deconstruct and cede its layers to the sea.

West to East

This hill is easterly. It greets the day with graceful golden ribbons that enlighten the environs. It has little in common with the foggy western hill, a mass of green sticks rising from nominally pacific waters. That hill is not present. That hill occupies foreign space.

At the base of that hill, when the particulate poison dissipates and the dark air turns translucent, a northbound mirage reveals postcards of downtown skyscrapers. Broad-brush strokes of Technicolor orange blur the showy urban artifacts. Left of center, nine mythological letters sprout from the hillside.

Turn around to see the bridge that sails into town from the east. Over that bridge, that hill meets a transitional main street with a trolley and a majestic theatre of dramatic arts.

Turn around. Spin. Spin and spin and spin and spin. Spin until the cycle becomes unbearable and dizziness ricochets into clarity.

Turn around to discover same with other. Turn around to see the bridge that hopscotches into town from the west. Over this bridge, this hill meets a transitional main street with a streetcar and a majestic theatre of dramatic arts.

In petitioning for legitimacy on this hill, one document is destroyed and another is assembled. The identifiable past is shredded into faceless fragments from a distant state of being. Decades of personal history are reduced to rubbish. License is granted to reconstruct an identity predicated on precision of place. Lucky numbers repeat in the shorthand of xx7 7th Street, NE, Apartment 7. Hope inhabits this hill.

Hope has journeyed from west to east to reach the avenue of independence that elevates this hill. This hill has unfinished business. This hill will fulfill.

Andrea Adleman is a political operative, communications consultant, journalist and food critic. Raised in the DC metro area, she returned to Washington after two decades in Los Angeles and now resides in the Atlas District on Northeast Capitol Hill.

Sketch 2 – Eastern Market
Marguerite Beck-Rex

RTE. 1 - OVERPASS TO FOUR MILE RUN
by Amy Young

Sunday, January 16, 2011

A thermal over the Gold Crust Bakery
catches the scent of Sunday's bread -
the air is exalted.

In the former railroad yard,
backhoes rest like sleeping swans;
warehouses and repair shops
form a low wall to the west,
while to the east the Potomac flows on.

At Jack Taylor's, Toyotas are tucked in tight,
trees trimmed in tear-drop lights.
Just over the bank by Four Mile Run,
five fishermen cast their lines
to the traffic's hum.

And over the asphalt sea
where barge-like box stores disgorge their goods,
gulls wheel in a carnival of gluttony.

*Amy Young grew up in Washington, DC and is a graduate of Wilson
High School. She lives in Alexandria and teaches at The Lab School
of Washington. Her poems have been set to music and performed at
the Smithsonian American Art Museum and she is Alexandria's
second poet laureate.*

TOUCHING DOWN IN WASHINGTON
by Patricia Gray

In cherry blossoms, I dream of Paris,
La Traviata bursting from the Opera house—
and like my mother's friend who wakes at 3 a.m.
singing La Marseillaise, I want a connection
that deep—perhaps to the Chat Noir, where
my body could paint the night in spirals
of crimson scarves.

Ah, Moulin Rouge, Degas, and decadence:
le petite body like glass, with us until broken.
In the study's soft light, my breath dusts
the Claude glass that once mirrored landscapes
for artists to capture with paint. Could
its dark surface picture a life, if angled right—
a life made miniature and manageable?

It's snowing in April in Washington. Lush
pink and white blossoms already engorge
our street, and like a French woman, I dress
in black pants, ballet flats, long scarf, and
large jewelry. How beautiful it is to walk
through falling petals mixed with snow,

then stop to view from the Capitol L'Enfant's
wheel of streets, their spokes reaching
to the west and northwest in this city I love—
the galleries and museums only steps away.
Washington is a graceful city, as the British
Airlines pilot noted the last time we
looped over Washington, before touching down.

Patricia Gray's *poetry collection,* Rupture, *was published by Red Hen Press. Her poems have appeared most recently in* Ekphrasis, Beltway Quarterly.com *and* Best of Potomac Review. *A former director of the Poetry office at the Library of Congress, she currently teaches at The Writer's Center in Bethesda.*

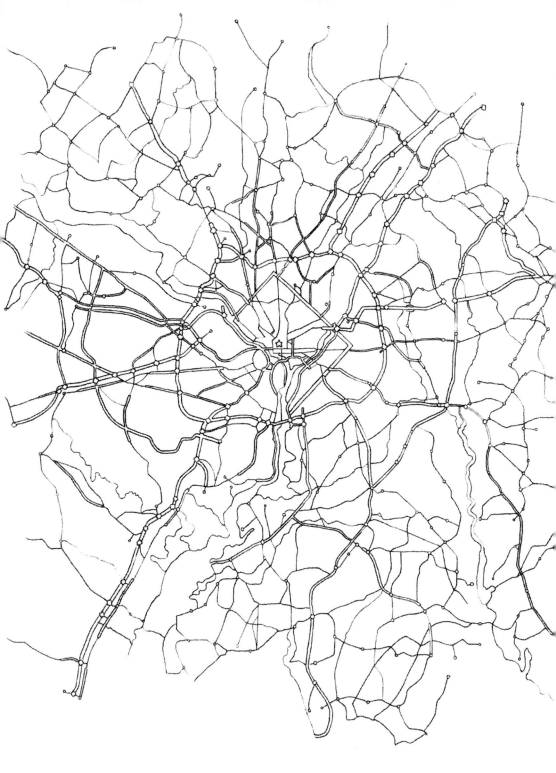

Constituents.

IN WARD FIVE THE CHILDREN GO TO FUNERALS
by Mary Ann Larkin

Stiletto heels.
That's what the girls wanted to wear
but the grandmas said no:
"This ain't no party."
The boys huddle together:
Dexter, Terence, Donnell
wanting answers no one knows,
not the grandmothers,
hymnals in their laps,
not the children high-fiving
as they enter the church,
nor the preacher, black-robed,
who dares not say: *I cannot save you*
nor speak to you of what devours you.
Afterwards, Marcus says
when he goes to jail
he'll come home toned:
"Ain't you noticed, Miss Maddie,
when the dudes come off the jail bus
how toned they all are?"

Mary Ann Larkin's *latest book is* That Deep and Steady Hum, *published by Broadkill River Press. She is retired from teaching at Howard University and has lived in Ward Five for 25 years.*

TRUE PLUMBING TALES FROM THE WHITE HOUSE
by Margaret Arrington

Being employed for over 30 years as a White House plumber, my husband Reds saw and did a little bit of everything, and it didn't always include plumbing.

Shortly after Truman took office, the White House was declared unsafe for habitation, so the First Family had to move across the street to the Blair House. Reds got a call that there was a leak in the President's bathroom. The water was coming from Margaret's bath on the floor above. The staff would not enter a room when the President was there, but good ol' Harry told Reds to come on in. As Reds was working, Truman said the water smells like "home brew." Because the water from the leak had been lying on the canvas ceiling for some time, it did smell funny. Truman also said "we are having a helluva a time with the places where we live."

President Eisenhower, the golfer, had a putting green installed outside the Oval Office. Soon squirrels, trying to bury acorns and other nuts, were tearing up the putting surface, which didn't sit well with Ike. The solution: trap the little critters and send them to the woods. Reds brought several to the forests of Mayo, Maryland.

When Queen Elizabeth was a visitor at 1600 Pennsylvania Avenue, a throne type chair was built to fit over the commode in her bathroom. Reds would joke, that was a true royal flush.

President Kennedy really enjoyed the swimming pools. Because he liked salt water, they tried adding salt to the pool water, but it didn't work out. There were no steps in the pool until the carpenters built some and Reds put lead in them to hold them down. Off the ground floor, in an air shaft, was a slop sink for mops. Often the pipes would freeze. Al, a plumber, took a torch to thaw them, but caught the insulation on fire. The smoke went up the ducts and into Mrs. Kennedy's closet. What a mess. Jackie was angry and probably all her clothing had to be cleaned. At least the fire department didn't have to be called and no one was fired.

Mrs. Kennedy wanted goldfish and ducks in the south fountain. The ducks found the fish tasty. Al, the plumber, a southpaw, opened the valves instead of closing them and all the fish went down the drain. Quickly someone went for replacements, but it was a losing battle.

Another time, Reds was cleaning the green slime from the bottom of the fountain with a fire hose, when Mrs. Kennedy, Caroline and John John came to watch. Apparently the first Lady wanted a closer look and climbed into the fountain at a place where the slime hadn't been hosed off. Her feet went out from under her and down she went. The secret service agent had her in an upright position before Reds could get there. Her clothes were covered with gunk.

Jackie decided the north and south fountains should remain on year round. Of course the jets froze in cold weather and caused a problem. The plumbers got a small aluminum boat from the Park Service, put it in the fountain and took a pole to break up the ice. The first time the President saw this, he said "I can't believe my eyes, someone is fishing in the fountain." Heaters were finally installed and the fountains continue to run all year.

Caroline had two hamsters. When they escaped from their cage, a posse of all available help was formed, but only one was located. Maude Shaw, nanny to the Kennedy children, called the plumbing shop to say that John John's diaper slipped from her hands and was causing flushing problems. Reds to the rescue, diaper retrieved.

Shower problems and lights out, are the five words that best describe the Johnson years. Much has been written about both. Reds worked on showers for the President from the White House to the Texas ranch. At least LBJ expressed his pleasure after five years of work and turmoil. That helped to ease the headaches and pain endured by the staff.

The Nixon family did not demand or require much. The President got rid of the Johnson shower and turned the pool into a press office. When Julie lost a contact lens in the sink, Reds was able to find it. The plumbers made the wedding cake holder and the stanchions for Tricia's wedding. Our family was invited to a church service held in the East Room. When our middle daughter shook the President's hand, she asked how his tooth was. An article in the paper had told of his toothache and trip to the dentist. President Nixon laughed and said it was fine now. Workers felt very sad when he left office.

The Ford's dog, Liberty, loved to swim in the fountains. The horror of all horrors occurred while the President was taking a shower. Someone digging by the fountain broke the water line, the flow of water stopped, and Ford had to go to his wife's bathroom to rinse off. No repercussions were felt.

The Carters demanded much more paper work than the other administrations. Reds was glad he could retire.

Tradition has it that on Inauguration Day, the new president will not move into the White House until after he is sworn in. During the two hours of activities at the Capitol, all White House staff is busy moving the old out and the new in.

Reds helped remove the awning when the Truman balcony was built. He went searching for corn stalks, when they were needed for Halloween decorations. When extra help was needed for moving furniture, helping with floral decorations, preparing for President

Kennedy's funeral or helping at state dinners, etc., all staff pitched in.

With the First Family away and work to be done, Reds would stay into the night. The big, old house was spooky when it was dark and quiet. Feeling devilish, Reds in the darkened Lincoln bedroom, with a flashlight shining on his face, started making weird sounds as one of his co-workers passed the door. He enjoyed remembering the guys high tailing it down the hall.

Taking care of the 32 bathrooms, in addition to the other duties at the White House, provided wonderful memories. Reds felt it an honor to serve seven presidents.

Margaret Arrington was born in Washington, DC, and moved to Edgewater, Maryland, in 1952. Her husband worked as the White House plumber from the Truman through the Carter administrations. This is her first published work.

FLIGHT
by Willa Reinhard

A warning bell chimed before the subway car doors slid shut, and Calvin leaned his head against his mama's side. Her fingernails brushed his low-cut hair—crown to forehead—in time with the train's low rumble. She had taken him to see the planes. For a whole month, ever since his fourth grade class took a field trip to the Air and Space Museum, Calvin had been begging to go back. He wanted to climb inside that real space ship they had, explore all through it; sit for a while in the pilot's seat.

It was a Saturday, his mama's day off, and the museum, like all of the Smithsonian, was free. They had arrived at the metro station across Constitution Avenue around one o' clock. It was April, the sun the only break in the blue, blue sky, and they bought two hot dogs, loaded up, two cold can sodas and a bag of onion rings to share. They sat on a park bench beneath a shady oak to eat, and made fun of the white tourists and the Chinese who were running around the Mall, looking all out of place, snapping so many pictures of nothing.

"Look at her," his mother pointed at a woman, skinny as two sticks, short red hair rising from her head like a rooster's crown. She shot across a grassy patch grabbing for two scattered children, trying to get them to mind her. When the rooster-headed woman skidded to a halt, Calvin and his mother looked where she was looking, at a group of three black boys walking nearby, fresh sneakers, jeans sagging, over-sized polos that matched the accent color of their shoes, and fitteds; the price tag dangling from the hat's brim like a flag.

"Up to no good," said Calvin's mother, sucking her teeth and sucking up the last drops of soda through her straw. Calvin wished his older brother Darren had come. He was seventeen and spent most days perched on a low brick wall on Delaware Avenue in SW, two blocks from the apartment where they all lived. "That ain't my style, little man," he had said the last time Calvin invited him to a movie he and his mother were going to see.

"Ah, look at that boy's pants," said Calvin, elbowing his moth(pulling her eyes to another tourist who looked straight from the c(fields with high-water jeans, faded and out of style. She giggled with Calvin. The three black boys loped on, the dip and rise of their stride indifferent, as if they had no idea that a woman had lost her breath because of them.

Now, it was almost six 'o clock. The green line shuttled from L'Enfant Plaza toward Waterfront station, and Calvin's mind settled on another boy he'd seen. That white boy; that boy who set himself up right in the middle of the room where projections of fighter jets and helicopters flashed fast as anything, transforming a simple white wall into a real live battlefield. Calvin sat beside his mother, on the designated stools, to watch the fifteen minute film, but that boy, Calvin's same age, had sprawled out on his stomach, knees bent behind him, shoes edged off and dangling from the very tips of his toes, head lazy on two fists. That white boy sat so close to the screen it must have seemed like he was fighting that fight, like it was him flying those planes. Calvin had kept his eyes glued on that boy, laid out that way, like he was nowhere but home.

At their apartment building, Calvin followed his mother up four flights. She dug through her purse for her keys, her black hair dropping in long coils so the red streaks showed in turns. She looked pretty today. She had worn a green cotton dress, bright as leaves and flouncy where it hit her knees. "I had a good day," said Calvin, and a faint smile danced across her face before she stepped inside.

Tomorrow morning when he woke up, his mother would already be at Shoe City, and then she'd make her way to the downtown office building she cleaned. He wouldn't see her again until she ducked into his room to kiss him goodnight, would not see her again for real until next Saturday, when she was off again.

"Darren," his mother called out loudly, hooking her purse around the back of one dining room chair. "Dar-ren!"

"That boy ain't here!" Calvin's grandfather yelled from the back bedroom, where Calvin knew he sat, stiff and upright, in his brown, corduroy recliner, studying his chess board. In the living room, Calvin watched, bug-eyed, as his mother strode down the short hallway to the bedroom her two boys shared. He hated when she acted like this. She had seen Darren, same as he had, out there hustling where he always was. They had walked right by him and his boys on Delaware. Calvin had lifted his chin upward in recognition, but his mother and brother didn't speak.

The rest of the evening, his mama clanged around the kitchen, banging rice and fish onto three plates without a word. "Food," she yelled, "and ya'll got the cleaning." She took her dinner into her bedroom, shut the door behind her, and soon Calvin heard her TV buzzing. That was how the day ended, one minute passing and then another until all the good things in it disappeared.

It was still dark when Calvin awoke to the sound of the front door shutting and his brother's heavy footsteps.

"Five o' clock in the goddamn morning," came his mama's voice, heavier than Darren's feet. If Darren responded, it was nothing he could hear. "Soon it won't be no door for you to walk through. Keep thinking I'm playing." His mother sighed so hard Calvin thought she could have exhaled her whole body through her mouth, and then the front door opened and closed as she left. When the doorknob to the bedroom clicked open, Calvin pretended to be fast asleep, but he listened for the sound of his brother undressing and for the creak as he lay down in the other twin bed. When Calvin woke again, the sun slid through the sides of the drawn shade, the covers were pulled back and Darren was already gone.

***

At school, Calvin scored ninety-eights and one-hundreds in science and math, easy as catching summer fireflies, and every Friday he walked home with a spring in his step, his backpack aglow with graded papers. In the first week of May his teacher, Mrs. Mosley, who was new to the school, called his mother at her night job to tell her about a camp called Imagine for smart kids. "It would be so good for him to be among his academic peers," Mrs. Mosley had told her. "They offer full scholarships for inner-city youth." His teacher wore her hair in dreadlocks that grew

35

long like copper vines down her back; she had once lived somewhere in Africa and was the type to show up at a student's house unannounced, asking why no homework was getting done. This had only happened twice that Calvin knew of, once with his friend Tyrone Gates, but it was enough to earn her a reputation. Some of the kids started saying "why she always be trippin'" and calling her Mrs. Motherland behind her back. But Calvin liked her. The Saturday after the phone call, his mother sat in bed flipping through the glossy brochure Mrs. Mosley had given Calvin to bring home.

"I could take Flight Science," said Calvin, on his knees, hovering over her while she read. The radio on her dresser played WKYS 93.9 and "Teach Me How to Dougie" came on. He would take a single class, five hours a day for four weeks. The camp was overnight, located near Lynchburg, Virginia, four hours south of DC. There was swimming, basketball, and dodge ball in the evenings, a dance every weekend. Calvin bounced on the mattress, shaking his shoulders to the radio.

"Boy, you'll be crying before the first day is over," said his mama.

"Na-uh! Four weeks ain't long," said Calvin, grabbing the tops of her bare arms, twisting her shoulders to the music.

"Maybe not." She swung her legs off the bed to put on her slippers. "I could try to get off. Borrow someone's car."

Three weeks later, Calvin received an envelope in the mail congratulating his acceptance. When he showed Mrs. Mosley, she hugged him tight, her skin smelling like earth after the rain.

Calvin was to leave for camp the last Sunday of June, two days after school let out. "What you know about them white boys?" his friend Tyrone asked that Saturday as they hid behind a clump of bushes five blocks from home, flinging rocks at cars passing down M Street. His mama was at work. She switched shifts with another lady so she'd be able to take him the next day. They would leave first thing in the morning.

"Them white boys can't *see* me," said Calvin, posturing, punching his right fist into the hook of his left palm.

His mother didn't like him playing with Tyrone, all gap-toothed and angular; limbs spindly as a spider's. He kept his hands busy in what

36

wasn't his, she said, and one of these days that was going to get him in trouble. Tyrone aimed for a rusted red pick-up; his rock barely hit the silver back fender. Most of the rocks they slung were quarter-sized, their targets already beat-up. This made it feel like more of a game for them, no harm, no foul.

"Won't you see *this* then," said Tyrone, handing Calvin a rock his fingers couldn't fully close around as a battered station wagon lumbered around the curve.

Calvin slung the rock hard. It banged against the lower half of the back passenger window, a sunrise cracking across the horizon where aluminum met glass. The driver swerved to the curb with a screech. The boys ducked down; heard the slam of a door before a man, burly and dark with a mottled face emerged. His curses coated the air behind them as they sprinted through the bushes like track stars.

Back on Delaware, feeling confident they were in the clear, the two friends split up. On his way home, Calvin passed his brother macking on a girl. Darren leaned back against the low wall where he always was wearing dark grey sweatpants and a wife beater that showed off his muscles. His right shoulder was inked with a large, black cross intersecting a large D. His forearms, the left tattooed with Gothic lettering that spelled "*And what?*" rested on the girl's hips, familiar, like they had always been there. She looked good, a sheen to her medium-brown skin, as she stood in the V of Darren's legs, dressed in a bright pink tank top and booty shorts, her full behind cupped in Darren's hands, as if that, too, had always been the case. "My brother is the man," thought Calvin, darting by, feeling just then like the two of them were invincible.

The next morning, things went badly right away. Calvin was cramming the last of his clothes into a large duffel bag when his mother came in and sat on the edge of his bed. He had gotten up on his own at 7 a.m. so he would be ready to go by 8 a.m.; registration ended at the camp at 2 p.m.; his mother wanted to leave early in case there was traffic or an accident or some other unexpected emergency. The night before, on her way home from work, she had picked up her girlfriend Dionne's car. But now it was 7:53 and here was his mother on his bed dressed in the t-shirt and shorts she slept in.

"I can't take you, baby," she said, her eyes reaching. The manager from her night job had called her in; two people were out sick; there was a big conference beginning Monday; an outdoor concert today. The building and plaza surrounding it had to be cleaned. "I'm sorry." Her face was plain and tired.

"You have time," he said, wanting her out of his room, changed into street clothes and ready to walk out the door with him. "You could get back in time, Ma." Her shift started at 4 p.m.

But she was steady talking about traffic, saying there was no guarantee, promising she would find somebody else to drive him.

"I don't *want* nobody else!" yelled Calvin, hating her.

She smacked him hard across the back of his skull and then once more for good measure, saying he must be a fool and maybe he ain't need to be at no camp if he planned to act a fool. She left him on the verge of tears, and Calvin ran outside, thumping his duffel behind him down the stairs, his skin wide awake with her palm.

By two o'clock, his mother still hadn't found anyone and Calvin sat on his bag on the steps of his building, brooding, refusing to even look at her as she walked in and out the front door. *You ain't trying*, he felt like saying, but he wasn't fool enough to get smacked by the same hand three times in one day. An hour later, she sat down next to him, dressed in the beige polyester pants and button-down that was her uniform. "I asked your brother," she said, and Calvin wouldn't look at her. He stared straight ahead where some of the older women from the neighborhood, Miss Pat, Miss Darlene and Miss Mable passed by, along with some others whose names he didn't know. Their church hats colored the overcast sky, topping fresh hairdos like exotic birds on the brink of flight. Their husbands trailed them like shadows, wearing darker shades, only Mr. Edwards bold enough for pinstripes and a red necktie.

"He was the last one I could think of," said his mother. "I gave him Dionne's keys against my good sense. See if he decide to do something right for a change." She waited for Calvin to say something then pushed herself up off the step and headed toward the sidewalk where the church women and men had just passed and then she paused and called his name sharply. He looked at her. "I hope you go," she said. Calvin maintained his silence, and his mother headed off right, in the opposite direction of the women and their hats, toward M Street to the subway to downtown.

Willa Reinhard is a DC native. She received an MFA in Fiction from the University of Miami in Florida and has been awarded fellowships at the Virginia Center for Creative Arts and the Ragdale Foundation.

AUTUMN LEAVES
by Shanti Chandrasekhar

Now it's on. Now it's off. One day we chat for four straight hours – sharing our innermost feelings with one another – the next day we're barely on talking terms. Lately, there have been more next days, though. I do not know if I can take it much longer. I try to laugh it off, blaming it on our hormones.

Jessica, what is going on?

I've probably written half a dozen emotionally charged what's-wrong-with-us letters to Jessica, but never sent her one. They remain buried in the pile of grocery lists, coupons and bills on my kitchen table. My kitchen table – the disorderliness that makes my husband cringe.

"Mom! It's Liz. She wants me to go to her house. Can I go, Ma? *Pleeease…?*" I glance at Mili standing on the stairs – each foot on different steps – one hand holding an open book and the other her cell phone, with just her elbow resting on the railing to balance herself.

God, don't let her fall!

"Now? It's almost six o'clock, Miloo!"

"Please, Ma, just for a while? And it's Fridayyy…."

I look at my beautiful daughter; at her sharp features, her brown eyes with long and curved black lashes that proclaim, "who needs mascara?" And then I notice the apprehension in her eyes, just waiting for an affirmative reply from me.

"OK."

"Yesss!" she hisses. "Hey, Liz! I'll be there in ten minutes."

"Who said anything about 'ten minutes'?" I ask. "I'm in the middle of cooking, sweetheart."

Mili is already halfway up to her room to get whatever she needs to carry to Liz's.

Liz is her best friend. Jessica's daughter. My best friend's daughter.

I cover the chopped onions and tomatoes with a soup strainer. Thank goodness I did not start sautéing them yet. Every evening, I spend a couple of hours in my kitchen—chopping, grating, grinding, and cleaning. Indian cooking is awfully time-consuming, I complain to Jessica, who just *fixes* dinner 15 minutes before her family sits down to eat.

"Something smells great in here!" all parents remark when they enter my house to pick one of Mili's friends up. With a smile, I make the standard suggestion to the standard remark, "You should come over and have dinner with us sometime." The waft of garam masala in every corner of the house that embarrasses Mili when her non-Indian friends visit apparently has the opposite effect on the parents. They respond to my suggestion with a "Sure, we would love that!"

Not as if it really happens. Even if I try to be the typical, hospitable Indian woman, not all our American and Asian acquaintances feel free enough to come over and chat with my family at the dining table. Except certain friends like Jessica. Jessica even reaches for whatever leftover Indian food I have in the refrigerator when she ends up at my place on a weekend after a tiring day of running errands.

I look around to see if I can get done with something more within a minute, before Mili is ready to leave. I taste the spinach before I turn the stove off. Salt. I shake some more salt into it. The rajma is not done yet. Had it been ready I would have poured some into a Rubbermaid container for Steve. Jessica's husband just loves the beans I cook. He calls everything "Indian beans," whether I make rajma with red kidney beans or cook garbanzo beans and call it chhole.

"It's not worth it, Jess," I once said to her, when I first sensed some uneasiness between us. "Nothing is. Just think, Jessica. It's one thing to have close friends when you're in your teens or twenties. But to find a real friend at our age...." I paused, waving my hand with a helpless gesture. "Nothing should spoil our friendship."

"Oh my God, Meghna!" She squeezed my hand and assured me then, "Nothing ever will."

Oh, really? Then, how come when I stop by to pick Mili up, I get the feeling she wants me to leave right from her foyer? How come I can't just walk into her kitchen anymore and chat over a cup of coffee? No, we don't do that anymore. Now I drink my brewed coffee all by myself and brood over things that drive me crazy; things like: how can I change a grown-up's attitude? Why can't a 40-year-old act like one?

I hear Mili racing down the stairs. I grab my keys and we step out. In the car, I remind her that she needs to work on her Fitzgerald project this weekend.

Mili and I had visited the St. Mary's Catholic Church Cemetery where F. Scott Fitzgerald's remains are now buried. Mili wanted some pictures and details for her presentation. When she found out the cemetery was at the intersection of Route 355 and Veirs Mill Road, less than four miles east of our home, she was surprised that we live so close to the historic site.

"Did you tell Liz about the project?" I ask her as I slow down, approaching a red light.

"Yeah, I did!"

I will not be surprised if the next thing I hear is that Jessica plans to drive Liz to the Lincoln Memorial for some project. Before I make a conscious effort to stop my thought process, I hear Mili say, "And I told her about *The Great Gatsby* inscription on the tomb. And Liz was, like, that's so cool!"

"Stop saying 'like' – you write so well, what happens to your language when you speak?"

A sideway glance and I notice her pout. I smile and reach for her hand. I know what will cheer her up. I start quoting the words from Mili's favorite book – the inscription on the shared tombstone over Fitzgerald and Zelda's graves – and she joins me at the fifth word: "So we beat on, boats against the current, borne back ceaselessly into the past."

We don't go jogging or bike riding anymore – Jessica and I. I miss those outings, when the two of us enjoyed working out together even as we complained about fat thighs. She is now extremely busy with work after her promotion to the management position. This summer, had we gone on bike rides, I would not have complained as much. Having bought six pairs of capris, I put all my shorts away. Out of habit over the years to have Jessica look at the latest addition to my wardrobe after a trip to Montgomery Mall or Tysons Corner, how I waited to show her my new capris and tops from Nordstrom's half-yearly sale.

I never got a chance.

"Eight O'clock max," I warn Mili as I drop her off. I know she will not be back before 10 p.m. She'll end up having dinner with them, I am certain.

Although I enjoy the cool October evenings, today is too windy for my liking. I wish Mili would zip her fleece up. She's not looking at me. She is already talking animatedly to Liz, swinging her little backpack. She has shot up this summer and now is almost as tall as Liz. Unlike Liz though, she gets her height from her father. Liz looks more like Jessica, tall and slim and blue-eyed. The blue-eyed blonds, I tease them affectionately. Jessica's Buick Terraza is not in the driveway, I notice. I wave to Liz and Steve and drive away.

An hour after I drop her at Jessica's, Mili calls to tell me Steve will bring her home after dinner. Then my husband calls to let me know he is caught up in a meeting and that they have ordered pizza for dinner. That leaves me – might as well have some leftovers and save the food I cooked for the next evening.

As I open the Pyrex dish with the previous night's vegetables, I think of Mili and Liz. They are alike in so many ways: smart, talented, mature for their age – perhaps being an only child makes them grow up faster; and they are both such pretty girls. Why, my Miloo – so light-skinned – could probably pass for a white American. But she is not one. And to this day, Jessica believes that is why Mili got into the International Baccalaureate Program at Richard

Montgomery High School and Liz did not. For these programs in Maryland public schools, she insists, they like to have a proportional mix of all races.

Stop it, Jess! Even if that were true, you can't hold it against me.

What a relief – issues like who performs better at what, who gets more certificates at the school awards assembly, and who gets into which program do not come between the girls.

The bowl of leftover cabbage curry has stopped rotating in the microwave. I ignore the five beeps.

I wish I could ignore the little scars that have marred my once-beautiful friendship with Jessica. I whisper Jess's favorite lines from a poem I wrote for her birthday three years ago.

> Every grown woman needs
> someone with whom she can giggle like a girl,
> someone with whom she can share her hurt,
> someone with whom she can be herself.
> Every grown woman needs a friend.
> Like you.

I look out of the window at the bare trees visible in the moonlight. I look at the leaves on the ground. Dried, withered leaves that looked green and strong and beautiful not too long ago…

Seasonal leaves.

Shanti Chandrasekhar*'s short personals essays have appeared in* The Washington Post *and* Parade Magazine *(online). She lives in Montgomery County, Maryland.*

WITH BAISAO ON THE HILLTOP
by Terri Merz

With me, here, at Healy Circle
is Old Kyoto's humble Baisao,
and stiff, unsmiling Secret Service,
their ears attuned to visible wires.

Since all traffic's been brought to a halt,
I read about your pure jade sencha;
unseen, above, a circling hawk,
unmoved by your - or any – knowledge.

The library's voluminous riches,
being, for reasons of state, delayed,
I sip, Baisao, your poems of "suchness,"
happy to wait on a lovely day.

But now old Healy's granite welcomes
the just-arrived President of Kosovo:
brilliant in blue, a striking woman;
snapshots flash, almost in unison.

All this pomp dissolves in a moment.
and crossing the lawn, I see the hawk:
wheeling, turning, it lands near a chimney,
reaching to meet it, there, a young beak.

*Terri Merz was the co-founder and co-owner of Chapters Literary
Bookstore, which operated in downtown Washington, D.C. for 22
years, and she subsequently co-founded its 501 (c) (3) nonprofit
successor, Chapters Literary Arts Center.*

GOOD HOPE ROAD
by Richard Peabody

The gospel lady who called
for the book buy in Southeast
had taught piano lessons

and owned more sheet music
than I'd ever seen before or since.

Sellers always tell you
"I have a lot of books."
Yet rarely do they own more

than one semi-empty, knickknack
paddy wacked free-standing bookcase.

My helper had as many (if not more)
tats than Harvey Keitel in The Piano.
Elaborate Maori ink that wrapped

down one arm, clipped an ear,
and covered his sharp features

like kudzu swallows Carolina red clay.
Zeke hefted boxes out to the van and

I cut the well-meaning and sweet gospel
lady a larger than normal check. And then
I drove from Skyland to the Shrimp Boat.

We ordered mumbo wings and trout sandwiches
and ate while Zeke shared how much he loved

smoking Crack and Angel Dust cocktails.
I studied the pink fingerprints the hot sauce
was sculpting into my forlorn white bread.

Still amazed that the gospel lady had owned
almost nothing beyond her Aerosonic stand-up piano
whose yellowing keys clashed with her wallpaper.

She'd been pretty wary about opening her door
when she saw Zeke and his red and blue tats.

Told me she was letting the sheet music go
because she was getting glaucoma and
besides, she knew all of that music by heart

after teaching in the DC public school system
for more than 40 turbulent years. I wished

I could have cut her a larger check. And was
sorry I didn't ask her to play something for us,
some music that might have soothed Zeke's

death metal soul, or might have made me feel
less than a carpetbagger on her side of the river.

Richard Peabody *is a native Washingtonian. He has two new books out—a book of poetry,* Speed Enforced by Aircraft *(Broadkill River Press) and a book of short stories,* Blue Suburban Skies *(Main Street Rag Press). He has edited* Gargoyle Magazine *since its founding in 1976.*

TAKE YOUR MARK
by Michelle Brafman

Charlie Foote thought that he'd accepted his son Cody's extraordinary averageness. Cody had neither dazzled the admissions director at Sidwell nor shown enough aggression or speed to play travel soccer, and Charlie had admonished his wife, Jillian, when she'd dressed a younger Cody and his sister, Emma, in Dartmouth sweatshirts (Classes of 2022 and 2020 respectively) for their annual Christmas card photo. The Ivies weren't in the cards for Cody. Everyone knew that. Or maybe they were, if he continued on his unexpected path toward swimming excellence.

Cody's gift was discovered on a muggy June afternoon. With a few hours to kill before collecting Emma from soccer practice, Charlie had taken him over to the pool, a modest community swim club tucked into a wooded Bethesda neighborhood. Charlie had rarely made it to the pool during the years he'd toiled away for a D.C. boutique tax law firm, but that all ended the previous January when Oliver Quinn, whom he'd hired and mentored, laid him off. Oliver had the audacity to yawn mid-sentence, and that's what had hurt Charlie the most.

Charlie staked out a chair too close to the women Jillian had palled around with before her catering business had taken off. Clad in their yoga gear, they chatted easily while arranging carpools, tennis games, and Pea Pod deliveries on their iTouches. Charlie could have peeled off his trunks and taken a big crap on the pool deck, and they wouldn't have looked up from their screens. He thought to remind Cody to use sun block (Cody had inherited Charlie's ivory skin as well as his weak chin). Never mind, the sun was fading, and he didn't want to embarrass the boy. Cody caught Charlie staring at him and gave his father the smile that used to melt every artery in his heart. Now it only served as a reminder of the boy's desire to please, and pleasers don't get ahead in this world. Pleasers ended up pudgy and unemployed, eavesdropping on yoga lionesses dining out on a mom who was timing her daughter's workout swims with the stopwatch function on her iPhone, the woman's unbridled competitiveness making them feel better about their hefty investments in their kids' swimming. Maybe if Charlie had possessed this kind of intensity, he would have successfully sharked around the waters of his firm.

After a couple of games of Sudoku, Charlie glanced toward the pool and noticed Cody swimming the breaststroke. Four games. Five games. He looked up and Cody was still swimming. He paddled through two adult swims, a visit from the ice cream truck, and two diving board infractions. A broad-backed brunette in a sporty red bikini approached Charlie and introduced herself as Zoe, the new head swim coach.

"Normally we don't let kids swim during adult swim, but we were all so blown away by your son that we let him keep going." Zoe went on to explain that Cody's morphology—the hyper-extension in his knees and ankle flexibility—made him a natural breaststroker. Both Cody and Charlie's knees bowed back when they stood, forcing their bellies to jut out and their backs to sway, a stance Charlie had always attributed to low muscle tone.

"Do you think he would be interested in joining the swim team?" she asked.

"These kids have been swimming for years. Isn't he a little old to start a brand new sport?" Charlie heard the preposterousness of his concern; Cody was only 13.

Zoe laughed. "Breaststrokers are born, not made. He could pass up his peers in no time."

In a county heavily populated with gifted children who persistently identify themselves as such, Jillian could not hide her delight in learning that her Cody possessed a God-given talent. She promptly went online and ordered him a Speedo. For the next two weeks, Charlie dropped off Emma at soccer practice and took Cody to the pool. The night before the first meet, an intra-squad competition between the boys and the girls, Charlie asked Cody if he wanted to join a group of swimmers who were camped out at the picnic tables at the far end of the pool, tie-dying team shirts and eating copious amounts of baked ziti. "Nah," Cody said, and Charlie was relieved that his son had spared them both an evening of failed attempts at small talk.

"Can we watch a Columbo tonight?" Cody asked.

"You bet." Charlie tousled his son's wet hair, unsure if Cody liked these DVDs or if he watched them to keep his dad company while Jillian made obscene amounts of money as the official "go-to" caterer for people with food allergies, and Emma hung out in downtown Bethesda with other girls with silky manes and perfect jeans, girls Jillian referred to as Queen Bees with a hint of pride. Cody was a likeable kid, but he lacked the initiative to make new friends.

The next morning, Jillian was catering a bar mitzvah, so Charlie dragged Emma out of bed at seven o'clock, and they all drove to the pool. The theme for the boys team was Spartacus, and Zoe's assistant coach, Harrison, who did resemble a young Tony Curtis, greeted them with fake blood dripping down his hairless chest. Cody fought his way through the crowded warm-up lanes and hung in the back while Zoe and Harrison led the team cheers, their voices bouncing off the water, through the oaks and pines, and into the open windows of the surrounding Cape Cods, split levels, and an odd McMansion. The sun burned through a patch of clouds, but most of the pool was shaded, and the swimmers shivered, swaddling themselves in their damp towels.

Charlie told Emma to put away her iPhone when they announced Cody's heat. Emma examined the line of boys. "Why is Cody swimming with the eleven and twelve year-olds?"

Charlie explained that since Cody's birthday fell the day after the cutoff for the summer season, he could swim with the younger kids. Without a shred of sibling rivalry, she said "well, that's weird." It was indeed weird that luck would befall Cody since Emma was the child who had been born with a golden horseshoe nailed to her pretty little hoof, the girl who had her pick between Sidwell, Holton, and NCS, and who in third grade, guessed the right number of jelly beans in the teacher's jar three times in a row.

The starter called the boys to the lip of the deck. "Take your mark," he said, speaking so closely into the microphone that it muffled his voice. The beeper went off, and Cody looked around before he dove in. The other swimmers had already cleared the flags by the time he entered the pool. While his competitors took a stroke or so under water, Cody popped right up after his dive. Charlie relaxed into the predictability of Cody's mediocre performance. As soon as Cody broke the surface of the water, however, he swam with authority. Plain and simple. By the end of the first lap, he was in first place. Zoe was right, he did have something wonderful going on with his kick. Cody's nautical grace left Emma and Charlie too stunned to cheer him on.

Cody's second lap was even faster, and by the time he hit the final set of flags, he was a good body length ahead of everyone else. He touched the wall and looked toward the other lanes with bewilderment as his competitors glided into the wall. High fives all around. Charlie experienced an endorphin release that trumped any buzz he'd ever copped from any illegal substance he'd ever ingested. He wanted to skip over to Cody and hug the hell out of him. Yes, skip, like a little girl.

Charlie walked over to Zoe and Cody, the water dripping down his legs and arms, his chest heaving up and down.

"I can't believe I won," Cody gasped.

"You're swimming in the 'A' meet next weekend, buddy." Zoe grinned.

Cody and Charlie looked at each other in disbelief.

"Just wait until I teach you how to start," Zoe clapped Cody's shoulder.

Boom. In the course of the 40-some seconds it took Cody to swim two laps of breaststroke, the Footes became visible enough to strut into any pool pasta party or Karaoke night with their heads held high.

When school let out for summer, Emma went off to soccer camp in Pennsylvania, and Cody started swimming two practices a day. Charlie welcomed the routine, after months of lost mornings putting out feelers and drinking too much Starbucks with fellow victims of the recession.

True to her word, Zoe taught Cody a racing dive and underwater pull, and he won the breaststroke race in the next four 'A' meets. Charlie bought a spiral notebook and tracked and charted Cody's times, as he'd done for Carl Yastrzemski's RBIs back when Charlie had been Cody's age and his father, a mathematics professor, had mistaken his ability to retain baseball stats for a gift with numbers. Cody's meteoric rise to swimming stardom created a mystique around him, and soon his teammates began inviting him to join them for post-meet sandwiches at Panera, where the yoga lionesses ferried him in their SUVs.

The Monday before the Divisional Championships, the sun was dimming, the pool was emptying of children, the ice cream truck had made its last visit, and Cody's new friends had gathered around a table after practice to inhale a sausage pizza. Cody was walking over to join them when Zoe flagged him down. She told him that he could make an All-Star time if only he could improve his reaction to the starting beep. Cody agreed to try "Reflex," an exercise that would help him improve his response.

He looked longingly at his friends while he followed Zoe, kickboard in tow, to the end of the pool. Two cranky lap swimmers, an older couple with sun-damaged skin on their chests, begrudgingly cleared a lane.

Zoe explained that she would give him the start command, and he was to try and dive in the water before she whacked him on the rear with a kickboard.

"Swimmers, take your mark!" Zoe's raspy voice deepened.

Cody coiled his body into the starting position, resting his head between his knees, poised to dive exactly when she said "go."

"GO!" she barked.

He waited too long, so she swatted him on the rear before he could dive in the pool.

"You can beat this board, Cody. One more."

Zoe stopped after a few more starts. Cody wasn't getting the hang of this. His friends put down their pizzas, and soon they were swatting each other with kickboards and talking trash about each other's reaction times. Nobody noticed when Charlie meandered over to the big plastic bin on the opposite end of the pool, swiped a kickboard, walked out to the parking lot, and put it in the trunk of his car.

When they arrived home, Jillian was opening a cardboard container of salmon she'd served at a luncheon that day.

"Sit, sit, sit...I want to hear every detail about your practice," she said.

Cody started to tell her about his potential All-Star time, and Charlie could tell that she was trying to pay attention but her mind was elsewhere. Charlie had become the driver and navigator of their domestic vehicle, and Jillian a well paying passenger.

"That's fantastic, Cody. What time do you think you'll swim?" Jillian asked.

Charlie could tell she was trying to figure out if she could sneak out to the meet while her crew set up for a bridal shower in Potomac that she'd booked months ago.

"Did you get to the drycleaners today, Char?" Jillian turned her attention toward Charlie as if she were running a board meeting.

He winced thinking about how Victor, his 85-year-old neighbor who still shoveled his own walk, had called him Jillian's "wife" this afternoon when he'd come up the walk holding a dress she'd stained while serving tomato-free spaghetti sauce. "It's in your closet. So, how was your luncheon?" Charlie asked politely.

"Gluten, nut, dairy, egg, and garlic-free." She reached for the heavy ceramic salad bowl, and Charlie noticed that her arms and shoulders had become ropy from the manual labor catering demanded. She reminded him of the fierce co-ed he'd spotted on the lacrosse field at Dartmouth, the one his father warned was out of his league, his subtle reminder that Charlie had only gotten into Dartmouth because of his old man's tenure. Jillian adored Charlie because he made her laugh. He'd also typed up her honors thesis, paced her for her first marathon, and now kept her books. Charlie found their recent flip-flopping of roles unsettling, yet an inevitable outcome of their coupling.

The Thursday before Divisionals, Jillian was out catering a dinner and Charlie ordered Chinese, which he and Cody ate on the couch while they watched the Nats game.

"So, do you think you can swim that All-Star time Saturday?" Charlie asked Cody casually.

Cody turned to Charlie, and his desire to please his father was smeared all over his face, the half-smile and eager eyes. "Sure, Dad."

Charlie cheered on Bryce Harper, trying to quell his desire to retrieve that kickboard from his car like a drunk would a fifth of vodka he'd stashed in the garage. He couldn't stand it. He'd just go outside and get the kickboard, and then he'd feel much better, he told himself. It didn't mean that he had to use it.

"Be back in a second." Charlie got up and used the kitchen exit to the garage. He opened the trunk of his Acura, tucked the mildewed board under his arm, and put it in the pantry.

"Want some ice cream?" Charlie called out.

"Is it ice free?" Cody asked, and Charlie could hear his shy smile, and perhaps a tang of resentment toward Jillian who'd gone from super-stay-at-home mom to Washingtonian Magazine cover girl.

"Smartass," Charlie laughed, reveling in his status as the primary caregiver.

Charlie scooped mint chip and vanilla into a bowl and carried it into the den. "So, what do you say we play a little game of Reflex?" He asked as if he were asking Cody if he felt like renting a movie or taking in a Nats game.

Spoon in mouth, Cody chuckled. "What, did you like steal a kickboard from the pool or something?"

Charlie walked back into the kitchen, grabbed the board, and returned to the den. "Sure did," he said with bravado.

"Dad, one problem. There's no pool," Cody said through a half laugh.

Charlie patted him on the back. "Just dive into the couch. That should work fine."

Emotions traveled across Cody's face like a cloud across a clear blue sky. Surprise, followed by pity, and finally that stubborn desire to please. He put down his ice cream and walked over to Charlie. Peach fuzz had started to sprout under his lip, and maybe all of that water had made him grow, because he now came up to Charlie's chin. He'd clear six feet one day.

Cody bent over and crouched over his toes, as Zoe had instructed him to do.

"Take you mark," Charlie bellowed.

Cody tightened up his muscles, ready to spring.

Charlie raised the kickboard in the air, sick with shame and disgust and something more powerful that was swallowing him up whole. "Go," he said. Cody was too slow, and Charlie nailed him before he could jump toward the sofa and away from the board. If Cody could beat this board, he could win Divisionals; he could be the only twelve and under boy to make an All-Star time this season. Cody bent over for another turn without Charlie having to ask.

"Take your mark," Charlie commanded.

"Go." This time Charlie swatted Cody harder, fueling the adrenalin that was pulsing through him.

The next turn, Cody's shorts morphed into a screen of blue cotton, in which Charlie saw the disappointment curled around his father's mouth when he'd found a lousy calculus exam Charlie had hidden in his backpack. The next turn, Charlie saw that prick Oliver's bored face while he'd fired him, and then Jillian's look of sympathy and pride when they'd met with the accountant to inform him of their new tax status.

Cody stood up. "Dad, I think I'd like to finish my ice cream now," he said softly.

55

"One more," Charlie said, ignoring Cody rubbing his lower back.

Cody leaned over one more time, his smile faded, his muscles quivering either from exhaustion or fear. Charlie raised the board back, and just as he was about to conjure another memory of his failure, a headlight appeared in his periphery, and a car door slammed. His arm was shaking now, and he was starting to sweat under his armpits.

In the moment before Jillian walked through the back door, Charlie caught his reflection in the window across the room. He barely recognized himself, kickboard waving in the air, wildness in his eyes, and his son bending over, waiting for life to kick him in the ass.

"Swimmers stand back," Charlie mumbled.

"It's okay, Dad. Just one more," Cody said, still crouched. His shirt had hiked up his back, revealing the elastic waistband of his boxers and the red mark of a bruise that would soon blossom.

Michelle Brafman has received numerous prizes for her fiction, including the F. Scott Fitzgerald Short Story prize and a Special Mention in the 2010 Pushcart Prize Anthology. Her work has appeared in the minnesota review, Blackbird, Fifth Wednesday Journal, *and* Gargoyle. *She teaches fiction writing at the Johns Hopkins University MA in Writing Program and George Washington University. She lives in Glen Echo, Maryland.*

COLLIDE-O-SCOPE
by Robin Ferrier

He lived in downtown Bethesda, where at night the streets were bathed in lights from the windows of busy trendy restaurants and quaint wine bars. Where singles and young couples strolled under street lights until well after dark. She lived in Rockville, where families and children played in the parks during the day, and the lights you would see at night were mostly in the windows of homes where families watched TV together or children did homework. About the only thing the two locations had in common was that they were in the same county and shared a thoroughfare. Other than that, she didn't think their two worlds could be so physically close, yet so far apart.

He was 40 and single, never married. He owned a condo in the heart of downtown where he could walk to dinner or a bar. He'd purchased it years ago when he'd been smart enough to know he should buy rather than rent, but still young enough to care more about training for marathons and stumbling home from a night out rather than keeping up a yard. During one of their flirty phone conversations, when she'd found it so easy to tell him so much about herself, he'd told her that he'd never moved because he'd never needed to. She considered it a choice made by someone who wanted weekends and evenings free. Unencumbered. Easy.

She was 36, divorced and had a three-year-old daughter and a dog. She lived in a townhouse. She'd wanted to move into a single family home from the moment she'd found out she was (finally!) pregnant, but her ex hadn't wanted the upkeep and responsibility – not even after he knew a child was on the way and they'd bought a dog that needed room to run. And now… now she couldn't fathom working a full-time job and caring for Sophia and her dog and a house, and, yes, the yard work. She would have loved giving them a bigger house and a yard to play in, but she knew that wasn't possible.

To compensate for the lack of a yard, she took Sophia out to fun places on their weekends together. The Glen Echo Park merry-go-round. The Gaithersburg Water Park. The Rockville Town Center fountains. And, if it was raining, the Montgomery Mall indoor playground. Sunday mornings were reserved for The Little Gym. On the rare nights that she and her daughter ate out, they almost always ended up at the local chili joint or pizza parlor, both of which were well-lit and filled with noisy families. On her "off" weekends, when Sophia was with her ex, she'd spend leisurely Saturday mornings at Barnes & Noble sipping a latte, eating a scone, and doing a crossword puzzle. Her afternoons would be filled with running errands to Target or Kohl's, both meccas for the budget-conscious. When she'd first gotten divorced, she'd thought maybe she would go to bars on her "off" weekends, but she'd quickly realized she didn't fit in that scene anymore. Clubbing was a sport for the young.

How he spent his weekends was a mystery to her – after all, she hadn't been single in more than ten years and back then she was in her twenties – but she imagined it didn't include fountains, slides, swings, and jungle gyms. As to what a weekend might be like for him, she could only imagine it unfolding in one of three ways: 1) blackout curtains and sleeping in, 2) beer, buffalo wings, and TV sports marathons – or sports in person – with his buddies, or 3) hanging out at trendy bars. Or some combination of the three. It had been too long since she – or any of her close friends – had been single so she didn't really have a reference point. Those three scenarios could be all wrong. But try as she might to imagine otherwise, she just couldn't fathom what a 40-year-old single, professional man did with his free time.

Her inability to imagine his day-to-day life, his dating life, was one of the reasons she was nervous about tonight. He had spent his whole adult life dating. He knew what to expect. What to do. And she didn't know what to wear on a date let alone modern dating etiquette. Which brought her here, slipping a brightly patterned dress over her head and sliding her feet into the blue wedges that she'd splurged on earlier that week. She tried to imagine him in her world, giving up trendy restaurants and responsibility-free weekends to hang out with a three-year-old. Because if things worked out, if they began seeing each other on a regular basis, his every other weekend would sometimes involve spending time with her daughter. And while she knew how much fun Sophia could be, she didn't know whether he'd feel the same. Sure, he'd said that her having a daughter didn't scare him when she'd first mentioned it. But she hadn't fully believed him then because he'd backed off for a while after that conversation. Who could blame him? That was when she wasn't even separated yet, just on her way there, spending too much time and money on the lawyer who was negotiating her future. And even now, with all the details ironed out, her life was still full of wrinkles. He'd see that soon enough if he stuck around.

She imagined his life was the opposite of hers. She imagined his life was smooth. Clean. Simple. How much muss and fuss could there be when you lived alone?

The truth was, she knew little about him other than where he worked and that he liked to read serious literature, his current choice being John Updike's *Rabbit Run*. She found his love of reading incredibly enticing, because she'd never been with anyone who liked reading as much as she did, and incredibly intriguing because it hadn't fit in with the picture she'd had of him in her head.

He hadn't told her where they were going that night. She wasn't even sure he considered tonight a date, though she did. Their plans had been instigated by her beating him in their March Madness pool. He'd seen playing against her as a great challenge when he heard from her co-workers that she'd won the office pool twice in the past three years.

"Seriously, how did you beat me?" he'd asked when the final game had been played. "You never even talk about college basketball."

"There are certain secrets that a woman doesn't share," she'd teased. "Besides, my methods aren't important. My prize is."

They'd made the bet with open stakes. Winner would name the prize after winning. He'd made the suggestion of the open stakes.

She'd hesitated at first. Then told him, "You know what? I'm feeling lucky today. You're on." He'd told her he wasn't usually a betting man, but he was in, too.

And now she'd won. As she looked in the mirror, she wondered whether the dress that she'd loved and had been saving for a special occasion was appropriate for the evening's plans. But she liked how it looked on her, how it hugged her curves in just the right way. She just hoped she didn't look like she was trying too hard. She'd never been so neurotic about dating, but then again, that was before she'd been through a difficult marriage and an unpleasant divorce. Before she'd spent that last year living with a man who didn't find her attractive or interesting.

She knew what she would have liked to have named as the prize, but if she ever got to kiss him – and make no mistake, she *wanted* to kiss him – she didn't want it to be because of a bet. She wanted it to be because *he* wanted to kiss her. So she'd named a much more innocent prize: drinks. Drinks could go anywhere, she figured. He'd countered that she at least deserved dinner with how soundly she'd beaten him.

He knocked on the front door, forcing her out of her head, which was a good thing. She knew she had a tendency to over-think things. She took one last look in the mirror and happy with what she saw headed for the front door. She knew that, if nothing else, she was attractive.

She opened the door and smiled. "Hi."

"Hey," he said back.

They hadn't seen each other in maybe six months, ever since his company had completed its project at her office. During that time, they'd emailed back and forth – moving their banter to personal email addresses instead of work ones – and spoken on the phone when she could use work as an excuse to call him. But their actual paths hadn't crossed.

She didn't know how to greet him, whether she should hug him or invite him in, so they stood there awkwardly.

"Do you want to come in?" she finally asked. "I need to find my purse."

"Sure," he said, following her into the entryway.

She searched the dining room for the purse she'd carefully packed only a short time ago, but couldn't see it with all the stuffed animals and kids' books covering every surface.

"Sorry for the mess. Sophia…" Her voice trailed off as she gestured toward the mess, seeing her house through his eyes. She felt a slight twinge of panic and insecurity. The Pottery Barn Kids chair seemed out of place both in color and placement. What had begun as a play area had spilled out into the living room despite her best attempts to corral the Little People toys and Legos. If he'd been trying to forget about her having a daughter, there was no escaping that now.

"You look really nice," he said to her back, distracting her from her momentary panic.

He couldn't see her smile in response.

"Thanks," she said.

It had been a while since a man had complimented her on how she looked. No, that wasn't true. She had an older co-worker who'd told her, as she was going through her separation and divorce, that one thing she should never question about herself was her looks. He'd told her that men would be like moths to a flame once she was "free." She hadn't believed him, though she'd always appreciated his compliments. Besides, his compliments weren't the same as hearing someone you liked tell you that you looked nice.

She spied the handle of the bag under a stack of mail and pulled it out.

"Ready," she said, turning back to him.

"Do I look like you remember me looking?" he asked.

The question caught her off-guard. She didn't know what had prompted it, but by the way he was playing with the collar of his shirt, she thought he might be just as nervous as she was. She couldn't believe he might be worried about what she thought of him. He had to realize he had the upper hand this evening. Didn't he?

"Yes," she finally said, realizing he was waiting for an answer.

"I mean, you usually saw me with a hat on," he said, gesturing toward his head and a thinning hairline that she'd known was there, but hadn't given much thought to.

It was the perfect opening for her to give her real response to his question. "Better," was what she wanted to say. "You look better than I remember," was the honest answer. But she couldn't tell him that. She didn't have the guts and didn't want to scare him. Plus, she didn't want to open up the possibility of him asking what she meant by it. It wasn't something she could easily explain because it had nothing to do with how he looked, really. He looked the same. It was more about the fact that she'd grown to know him and had become fond of him during their email conversations and flirty phone calls. And finding someone witty and fun and charming, well, for her, it always made someone more attractive. Not that he wasn't attractive in his own right, separate from his personality, but he might misunderstand her meaning. And she wasn't saying that at all.

"Should we go?" he finally asked, filling the silence that had taken over the room while she'd been once again over-thinking the moment. She nodded, and he held open the door for her. They walked to his Toyota Camry. It wasn't what she'd pictured him driving. She had taken him for a Lexus guy. Or at least an SUV. She wondered what music would come on when he turned on the car. She could promise it wouldn't be "The Backyardigans" soundtrack or Sandra Boynton's "Philadelphia Chickens" CD, both of which held permanent residence in her car's CD player.

"So I did a little research and there's supposed to be this really nice restaurant up near Sugarloaf Mountain called Comus Inn. Have you ever been there?"

"No."

"Me neither, but it seemed nice from the description. I got us a reservation for an outside table since it's such a nice night out. And there's a vineyard up there, too. We might have time to get a glass of wine there first. Does that sound okay?"

She'd been to Sugarloaf Mountain Vineyard before, often with neighbors, and a few times with her ex. But she didn't mention it because she didn't want the ghost of her divorce hanging over them tonight, ruining the evening. Plus, she liked the vineyard. She wouldn't mind making new memories that would erase the old ones.

"Sure," she said.

And it did sound… *nice*.

She wanted to tease him about how many times he'd used the word "nice" since arriving at her house. If they'd been having one of their flirty phone calls, she would have. But she couldn't summon that easy banter right now, perhaps because this was the first date she'd had in a very long time and she wanted it to go well. And he didn't know her well enough to know that her teasing him would have been a sign of affection.

She wondered if he was avoiding his usual hangouts because he worried she wouldn't fit in or was concerned about running into people who might not understand what he was doing with a 36-year-old single mom. Or maybe he was just trying to choose a place where he thought she would feel comfortable. She wanted to believe that he wasn't hiding her. That maybe he really was ready for a divorced mother and all that entailed. So that's what she told herself as he pulled the car onto the highway heading north. As he looked in the other direction, making sure it was safe to change lanes, she peeked over at his profile. Despite all the emails, she truly didn't know much about him.

But what she did know was this:

He was downtown Bethesda. He stayed up until at least midnight, a fact she only knew because when he emailed her, it was always that late. He lived in a hip part of Montgomery County that, in her mind, was inhabited by those who were single or had money.

She was Rockville. Many nights, after a full day of work and then caring for her family, she could barely keep her eyes open until 9 p.m. She lived in the heart of suburbia, surrounded by families and people with pets, and she lived on a budget.

While his nights likely consisted of sitting on a barstool enjoying happy hour with buddies, hers involved sitting on a swing and laughing with her daughter. But for tonight, she was putting all of that aside. Tonight they would sit across the table from each other, at a restaurant that neither one had ever been to before, in seats that she hoped both of them would feel were a good fit. And she hoped that maybe, just maybe, they'd discover their lives weren't as far apart as they seemed.

__Robin Ferrier__ holds an MA in writing from Johns Hopkins University. She has previously had work published in an anthology and the literary journal Gargoyle *and had a play performed as part of the Source Theatre Company's 10-Minute Play Competition. She lives in Rockville, Maryland.*

Sketch 3 – People Waiting for a Bus
Marguerite Beck-Rex

GOOD FRIDAY, 14TH STREET, WASHINGTON, DC

by Joseph Ross

He walked on raw toes
up the middle of 14th Street,
wearing part-dashiki, part tye-dye,
part army fatigues, part crazy.

His own way of sorrows
in the middle of Washington,
a place familiar
with crosses of all kinds.

He did not seem to see
the cars avoiding him
but with eyes of mercy
they saw him.

He seemed to be delivering
a lecture that was part sermon,
part symphony, part rant, part eulogy
to the grunting, blind city around him.

He spat as he spoke through cut lips.
He winced through neglected teeth,
evidence of deeper neglect.
His hands windmilled around him

in wild-eyed revolutions, loosening
his coats and scarves until he became
a flailing unto himself,
a calvary of arms and teeth.

Every now and then,
between the green light waves
of SUVs, I detect a few words
sliding from the altar of his mind:

Jesus, White House, Pentagon, Iraq.
Every syllable a night terror,
every saliva-glazed anger skids
onto every American

street, proving the point:
nothing is past, everything is now,
you don't always need a cross
and nails for a crucifixion.

Joseph Ross is the author of two books of poetry, Meeting Bone Man
(2012) *and the forthcoming collection,* Gospel of Dust (2013) *both
from Main Street Rag Publishing. His poems have appeared in many
anthologies and journals including* Poet Lore, Tidal Basin Review,
and Little Patuxent Review. *He is the 2012 winner of the Pratt
Library/Little Patuxent Review Poetry Prize. He teaches English at
Gonzaga College High School in Washington, DC.*

REMEMBERING EFFI
by Gina Sangster

I used to see Effi Barry on the number 30 bus that travels from far Southeast across town to upper Northwest and back: her elegant posture, somewhat angular features set in a mocha-tan complexion, her full head of hair carefully coiffed; a kind of Mona Lisa smile on her face, like she held a secret you might want to know. The wife of DC's reviled and adored former Mayor riding public transportation like anybody else. And if you've ever been on the 30 bus you know that it caters not only to young professionals working for Congress but to the poor and mentally ill who probably have a fear of the underground Metro system, preferring to stick with the familiar bus line that has carried folks around the city since DC. Transit was its name. In that mix of beleaguered humanity I sat across from Effi Barry and felt as though I knew her and understood her, though we never spoke.

Sixty-three is too damn young to die and her death definitely made me stop and think since she was less than 10 years my senior. You tend to notice people around your age in the obituaries, especially if you read them every day like I do, along with the rest of the *Washington Post*. It's a habit I inherited from my mother who would sit in her favorite chair by the window in her living room with a cup of coffee, reading the daily paper, including the obituaries. They are, after all, stories of our lives and you never know who you might stumble across: someone you haven't been in touch with in awhile, someone you care about from a distance. For me it's a kind of homage to the people of my hometown, to scan the names and photos; to stop and give a closer reading to a few that catch my eye. You may also discover things, like the fact that Effi Barry didn't know her father and that he was white, details that made me feel closer to her since I lost my father at 16. I learned she had been a model and worked in public health and later as a professor at Hampton University. Most people in DC at the time will remember her stalwart resolve in the face of her husband's trial on drug charges. She sat in court day after day knitting an afghan while the most sordid details of Marion Barry's addictions and womanizing were publicized, dissected and debated. He would later say of her, "In my darkest hour, she was my brightest light."

People around the world were grieving Pavarotti's death the same week Effi died. I glanced at his picture in the paper but it didn't take my attention away from Effi. I read both the obituary and a longer piece about her life, plus the announcement the following day that she would lie in state in the Wilson Building before a memorial service at the National Cathedral. I thought about asking one of my friends if they wanted to come with me to pay our respects along with hundreds of others for whom Effi's life had special meaning. The friends I thought of are divorced women like me and we've all stood by the men in our lives at different times for different reasons. I ended up staying at work that day, but my thoughts wandered to this woman I had never known but felt I understood. When I was getting divorced, some people didn't understand why I remained compassionate towards my kids' father; why wasn't I angrier at him for leaving? Why didn't I try harder to get more from him in a legal settlement? I know my mother's sisters said the same things, and worse, when she was putting up with my father's drinking and philandering. I've often said if my mother hadn't forgiven my father, I would never have been born. They remained together until he died after 25 years of marriage, sober and grateful to have us both. And even though my ex and I didn't reconcile, we continued to parent our three children, living ten blocks apart, and I know whatever resentment may persist is not fueled by a fire of my making. I believe Effi Barry triumphed in the end and that her silence was not acquiescence. She came back to the old neighborhood, held her head high and rode the Metro bus downtown with the people of the city she called home.

Gina Sangster *is a Washington, DC native who continues to live and work in her hometown. Gina has been writing since high school and has had a number of poems and essays published in literary journals,* the Hill Rag *and the* Washington Post. *Gina works as a therapist in Anacostia and in private practice on Capitol Hill.*

THE GREAT AMERICAN PEACE MARCH
on the National Mall
by Cary Kamarat

Ice-blue skies above the lawn,
sunwashed hooded mummers dressed
in orange and black, against the cold
the mocking dead stream by.
Barren trees sketch candied storm clouds.
Push and smile! and who's on bullhorn?
Just the press all caged in placards:
HAIRSTYLISTS FOR PEACE AND JUSTICE.
VETERANS FOR ONE MORE CHANCE:
See these boots? inquires the pundit.
Coulda been your son, these unclaimed
tags—no smiling glory story:
picture on the coffin, bunting
draped across a roll-roll wagon,
someone sings the red-white-blues.

The President's head in cardboard-mâché
drops away to show the throbbing
oil-drill pulse that drives the brain,
inside the blah-blah silhouette.
DC's Finest in their helmets,
star-dash blue and white at peace
with a rainbow crowd at a bristling barrier:
Gotta give the tourists room!
Gotta gi' duh drummuh some!

High atop the Towering Needle,
Bill and Sally and the children
all the way from West Sandusky,

look down at their favorite view
then askance, at two more hundred
souls awash at the needle base,
sitting, standing, shaping letters:
I – M – P – E – A – C – H.
Whoa! says Billy. *My!* says Sally.
Kids just watch the kite lines twang.

Horses spin to calliope rounds
jumbling bossa nova beats
from trumpet marchers, tuba dancers
up and down museum steps.
Oil-soaked grassroots press to lobby,
spearhead, coalesce behind
the Lofty Halls of the One Percent
that rule a New Banana Republic—
and yes, we have no bananas.
But jesters, fresh from writing checks
that roll like tumbleweed across
the lawn, now cry: *Please save our town!*
Evict the Congress, save DC!
There is another USA:
Thoreau, your boat so gently down!

And on one park bench lonesome, wizened,
camouflaged in shock, one jester
catches a moment's rest, his hand-drawn
placard, floating listlessly
above his hunter's cap, proclaims
simply, dryly, only, stop
oh
STOP THE MADNESS, PLEASE.

Cary Kamarat *is a teacher who has had poems in* The Federal Poet, Prospectus, Poets on the Fringe, *and on Israel National Radio. His photography has appeared in* The Tulane Review, *and both poetry and photography at www.travelwalk.blogspot.com.*

PERHAPS THE BIRDS:
Darfur Rally, Capitol Hill, Washington, DC
by Jean Nordhaus

Fling the emptiness out of your arms. ... perhaps the birds
will feel the expanded air with more passionate flying.
-   Rainer Maria Rilke

Azaleas, blossoming dogwood, demonstrators
straggling down the sidewalk toward the march
with the clear, virtuous faces of believers
on the way to church, carrying signs,
umbrellas, picnic lunches, collapsible chairs.
Everyone is happy, feeling good.
We are not lonely, not at all lonely now.
The weather is good and the crowd is large and we
are far from Africa. Perhaps somehow
these well-fed bodies, these ardent chants and songs
can alter the balance of darkness to light an ocean
and two continents away, can send
a little shiver of goodness out into
the world, can cancel the machete's swing

Jean Nordhaus's *two most recent books of poetry are* Innocence
(Ohio State University Press) and The Porcelain Apes of Moses
Mendelssohn *(Milkweed Editions). She is Review Editor of* Poet
Lore.

MY HUG-LOVING HOMETOWN, MY NEW AMERICAN DREAM
by Karen S. Zhang

"We all have different purposes when coming to America. Some people come here for work, some people for education, some for a good life, some others are for shelter," an Iraqi man said at a meeting in the public library to practice English. He eyed his thirty-something, scarfed wife by his side and continued, "We're fortunate to take refuge here in Virginia."

Specifically, he was referring to his new home in Centreville, Virginia, a town about 22 miles west of Washington DC. His words resonated with the audience sitting around the table. There were grandparents from Russia, a French teacher from Morocco, housewives from Korea, newlyweds from Honduras, a student from Pakistan, and a businesswoman from Peru. The room fell into brief silence after a vigorous discussion about where we came from.

Like the Iraqi couple, I am also a newcomer to Centreville. But the reason for my settling in this neighborhood is none of the above mentioned. Marriage brought me here. A year ago after my grad school in Pittsburgh, I followed my sweetheart to his Virginia home, a three-story corner town house in a peaceful residential development. From the house, I see wide roads crisscrossing one another, adorned with the changing colors of four seasons. Together with the dense canopies of trees and the high wood fences, the enclosed back yards often intrigue pedestrians to wonder what lies inside. Parked vehicles in front of rows of town houses, on both sides of the streets, and oftentimes in the driveway have shown me how many people have found homes in this lesser known suburban neighborhood near Washington DC.

For months, I had believed I was living in an unknown suburban area in America. Unlike Pittsburgh—the only American city I have lived in since I left my mother country China—with its fame of national sports and steelmaking history, few Americans are familiar with Centreville, Virginia. Unless I connect the dots with Washington DC or with the nearby historic battle ground—Bull Run, Virginia—people may exhale an "Oh yea!" after realizing the proximity. It is easier for me to tell my folks in China that I am living in Washington DC than getting into an arduous explanation about Centreville's location. After all, few back home know the geographic difference between Virginia and Maryland except that the White House is in Washington DC.

Centre-ville, in French means "city center." Yet, the Centreville that I find home feels more like a sprawling hub for capital region commuters. Unlike many cities, there is no town center, no municipal offices, and no designated business district with entertainment, restaurants and stores galore. Sitting on a ridge where spectators in the Civil War time once watched the battles of Bull Run, the city has a breathtaking view of the Blue Ridge Mountains. The long and flat mountain range skirts my horizon in the distance.

I was once told that people in America care less about where you come from but more about where you go to. Watching the incessant traffic flowing through the neighborhood, I can feel that the fast tempo of Washingtonians' life is ticking to the second. Everyone seems to be on the run. Perhaps sitting down for a cup of coffee is too much time to lose. Perhaps walking up on a moving Metro escalator is a signature of rushing metropolitans. Perhaps the pull of the destination outweighs the attractions on a commuter's journey. Perhaps this is the American dream that people are pursuing, a dream that brings people from all over the country and the world together to strive for.

No one will argue that a nation's capital provides the most secure jobs and stable life. No one will disagree that Washington DC is a multicultural city. Likewise, its peripheral areas welcome immigrants. Indians, Chinese, Koreans, Lebanese, Russians, Brazilians, Ghanaians, Salvadorans, Mexicans, you name them. Look, the staff workers behind the counter in my local post office are immigrants of numerous ethnic background—Iranian, Vietnamese, Korean, Bolivian. So are workers in the hospital, in the library and in the hotels. I am always lost in the tones of various languages spoken around me. But the undecipherable cadences have also reminded me of my being in a diverse Washington metropolis. When a friendly cashier greets me in Korean "an nyoung ha seh yo," I wish I could say something native to her rather than being tongue-tied.

A few weeks ago before daybreak, I went outside of my house to water the tomato plants as usual. This is how I like to begin my day. With stars blinking in the indigo sky and crickets chirping, the neighborhood was still in deep slumber. It was nearly unnoticeable to me in the dim streetlights when occasional vehicles quietly zipped by and early risers walked their dogs. As I was filling up the watering can, an elderly Asian woman walked up to me, trying to say something. She caught me by surprise. I stopped what I was doing and listened closely. Her rapid speech sounded foreign and futile. As soon as she saw bewilderment on my face, her eyes widened and her voice rose. She grabbed my arm and brought me closer to the tomato plants. She pointed at the leafy plants, continuing her indecipherable speech. She flailed her arms as if to show me the meaning of big. I thought nodding my head was a polite way to end such an unproductive conversation. Who knows why the elderly woman bent down on her knees and began pulling off the excessive leaves at the bottom of the tomato plants? After a few minutes, a pile of big green leaves lay on the ground like defeated soldiers.

"Beautiful," the elderly woman said after her unrelenting trimming of my tomato plants. She showed her hand gestured upward, suggesting the plants now would grow fast and tall. And most importantly, with *big* fruits. She closed her hands with a big shape of O.

"Beautiful," I repeated, assuming she might understand some English. I went on, "It's my first time to grow tomatoes. Thanks for your advice."

She nodded her head at the English word of "beautiful." But she spoke some more in her native tongue. Perhaps the rest of my words had puzzled her.

"Korean?" she asked, her eyes beaming.

"No, Chinese," I said.

"Chinese. Oh—" she sighed as if she had come to a revelation. She opened her arms and gave me a huge hug like a good old friend. She waved goodbye to me before she disappeared in the morning mist.

I had not got her name.

I am still shocked by that warm welcoming hug from a Korean neighbor. In Chinese culture, you don't speak to strangers, let alone give a hug to them. I used to think cultural differences create gaps among people rather than unite them. But in hug-loving America, an intolerable manner in my culture may become an approving norm. A simple "hello" to a neighbor may be the first step to gain your acceptance by the community.

***

For some reason, Centreville draws tens of thousands of Asian immigrants, in particular Koreans. Local businesses are mainly run by Korean American merchants. From restaurants to dry cleaners, from beauty salons to video shops, it is no exaggeration to call the city a Korean town. I have never been to Korea. But living in Centreville makes me feel like living in Korea. The Korean language can be spotted easily as if Koreans are showing a declaration of ownership. In addition to English, the store signs, the menus, and the imported Korean products sold in the supermarkets are written in Korean. Even the local library has Korean books on the shelves. No landmarks in Centreville are better known than the competing Korean supermarkets. As you walk in the in-store deli, the air is filled with the pungent smell of kimchi (a traditional fermented Korean dish) and many other Korean preserved goodies. From cucumber to radish, from cabbage to bean sprouts, Korean women prepare them with a variety of traditional seasonings. All these aromas mix together, making this customer's mouth water. On weekends, the food sampling is like a festival, drawing a big crowd. The sample stations display dozens of prepared delicacies with names that look foreign to English readers. Dynamic Korean pop music permeates every corner of the store. On the other side of the store, Korean-speaking customers are inquiring about the Korean cosmetics and herbal medicines. If only I knew Korean.

When I lived in Pittsburgh as a foreign student, the locals told me that the city had not attracted immigrants for years, so the local economy grew slowly. In other words, immigrants will help a town to thrive. Centreville is living proof. With appealing pricing, local businesses are scattered in the strip malls, competing with mega-retailers like Wal-Mart and Target. While politicians are touting their stimulus plan on domestic economy, immigrants have made a humble contribution to the new community that they call home. Until six months ago, it had never occurred to me to reach out to my community. I went to the library on the spur of the moment to look for possible jobs. In her forties, an Asian woman librarian at the information desk pulled out a form and explained to me in careful English several volunteer positions.

"At the moment, the library only has a few volunteer openings," she said. She passed me the form and continued, "If you're interested in volunteering, you may fill out this form. I'll leave it with the branch manager."

"Thanks." I said, struggling to believe that my Master's degree could not land a library job. "By the way, how do you like your job?"

"Not bad," the librarian said. She brushed her dark front bang as if stealing a few seconds for her to think about this abrupt question from a stranger. "I am glad that I can be of help to others. This is how volunteering fulfills my life."

"Are you a volunteer?" I asked. I had thought librarians are all paid.

"Yes. We have many volunteers working in the library. I'm sure you'll enjoy your volunteer experience like I do."

She is right. My understanding of the community is deepening. I volunteer to help people who are non-English native speakers to practice spoken English. People who come from all walks of life, who speak different mother languages, who have found homes in the neighborhood, or maybe are only temporary visitors, come together to learn to speak the same language, to share their commonalities and differences, and most of all, to build a sense of community.

That satisfaction is beyond words. Over the course of time, some participants have conquered fear to speak up in English, others have called English their own. I marvel at the courage the participants have taken to reach out. If it is not because of meeting them regularly, I would not have known how much I am yearning to make new friends, how much of my knowledge can benefit others. When they come to thank me for my help with their English, I say to them, "You've helped me to understand my community."

Centreville may be small but it reflects tens of thousands of little towns across the country established by generations of immigrants. At least to me, this is where my American residential life begins. When I first moved in Centreville, I was curious about the seemingly omnipresent Korean churches. Bilingual banners and signs are posted around the buildings. In fact, in every corner across the country where there are inhabitants, there is usually a church. The most striking architecture in any one-horse town is often a steepled church. Although Centreville is not a known historic town, its recent immigrants follow the same path to build churches, signifying the permanence of a settlement. As a venue for immigrants to share faith, churches are also where people can find a sense of belonging.

***

Years ago I heard about some overseas Chinese seniors having difficulty adapting to their new lives in America. In addition to language barrier, they had no friends and no emotional attachment to the community. Although I only have lived in Centreville for fifteen months, I gradually realize it is tough for an immigrant to survive in a foreign country. It is tougher if you choose to isolate yourself from the community. Perhaps this is why that senior Korean neighbor did not want to seclude herself. She came out of her way to show me how to grow tomatoes. Her big hug to me may be a sign of proving to herself that she has reached out.

Like people often say, except for the American Indians, everyone in America is an immigrant or a descendent of an immigrant. Perhaps this makes the value of building a community of love and care even higher in this country. Centreville may not have notable attractions but what it has are the down-to-earth and industrious immigrants who work hard to build a community. We have some experienced Korean hairstylists who can handle Asian women's tricky, long, straight hair. Korean style coffee shops often house a good collection of delicious bakeries. The Vietnamese pho bistro has a booming business, often crowded with returning patrons. There are a number of stores in Centreville selling ethnic food. Because of the convenience of doing Chinese grocery shopping, I sometimes have forgotten I am living in America. I often tell my friends jokingly that I have only moved from a large group of thirteen hundred million Chinese people to a much smaller Chinese community.

Although my Chinese appearance is often mistaken for Korean, my ignorance of Korean soon gives me away. The Korean names like Gooldaegee BBQ or Soo Won Galbi Restaurant often challenge me. It takes me months to remember a nearby Korean supermarket named "Hanaro." Just as I can say it right, the place is renamed as H-Mart. Changes in Centreville may be out of the league of China's rapid development. But the simple change in the ownership of a storefront or the periodical resurfacing of an old road always brings me a thrill. As the Iraqi man says, people have different purposes when coming to America. But we are all here to make a better life. With the influx of more immigrants, there will be even more communities around the capital region like Centreville, modest and thriving. There I see how our support for local businesses can invigorate the economy, how a modern community is built on a shared vision and open communication, and how my participation can add to the strength of the community. Perhaps, with a shared sense of community, this is a renewed definition of the American dream.

Karen S. Zhang*, a native of Guangzhou, China, now lives in
Centreville, VA. She received her MFA in nonfiction from Chatham
University in Pittsburgh, PA. Her essays and articles have appeared
in* Crazy English Speaker *and* Teens *magazines,* Coal Hill Review,
the Loyalhanna Review, *the* Times-Picayune *and the* Pittsburgh Post-
Gazette.

SUMMERTIME
by Diana Veiga

Ms. Angie swings her hips through the bar almost every night around seven o'clock. It's like she has some psychic powers because she always arrives in the doorway just in time to bump into the after work "just passing through crowd," make her way to the bar, and claim an empty seat before all the other regulars settle in beside her. Tonight doesn't seem any different because it's 7:02 and here comes Ms. Angie.

But tonight it's so hot, it feels like the devil is doing push-ups outside. I've been around the world and back on a boat, compliments of Uncle Sam, and one thing I know for certain is there ain't nothing like a DC summer. Even after the sun goes down, the air is still thick, seems to hang so low it almost touches the top of your head and grazes your cheek. And on top of that, our AC broke down last night, thankfully at the end of my shift. I thought they'd close the bar. I mean who would drink liquor in this heat?

But when I called this morning, the owner said, "Course we open. In the 40 years I've owned 'Ellavators at Petworth' I've only closed down Christmas and Easter – and that's only 'cause I don't think it would be right to be drinking on the days Jesus was born and rose up again. But any other day? We open."

Ms. Ella added the "at Petworth" part a few months back, and she keeps saying it out loud so it will stick. Apparently our neighborhood is "up and coming" and she wants to attract a whole new crowd. But to me, we don't need a fancy neighborhood name, this place is just home. And if you don't know that, then you shouldn't bother coming inside.

"But there's no air," I said, stating the obvious.

"Chile, please. People would drink on the sun if the price was right." I assumed as it usually does that her massive chest, that is always damp and sprinkled with flour cause she just threw some chicken into the fryer, heaved with every word.

So, now I'm here behind the bar, sweating my ass off – trying to catch a breeze from one of the three fans that's just pushing hot air from one corner to the other, and watching Ms. Angie as she comes through the heavy oak door.

She's a tiny thing, maybe a buck-twenty soaking wet. Tonight she's in her too short skirt- this one is silver with little sequins that damn near blinds you when the light hits it. Her white t-shirt, cut real low with the best of her breasts pushed to the top, barely covers her stomach so you can see it wrinkled and folded over her hips. She's wearing her usual metallic high heels that add about four inches to her small frame. And tonight she's chosen the short blondish colored wig. If she has to wear a wig then I prefer the longer red one with the bangs. But in all honesty she looks better with her real hair that's cut close and has a small, delicate curl.

I like when she comes in because she may be old but one thing she knows how to do right is walk. Not like these young girls who just put their ass up in the air like that's the only thing a man notices. No, Ms. Angie walks with her hips, lets them rock to a rhythm that must be playing in her head. She takes her time with it, walks like she ain't selling it, but she ain't giving it all away for free either.

Her skin is the color of almonds and you can tell that she was pretty back in the day. But now she has life all over her face – too much hard loving, drinking, working dead end jobs and chasing men with nothing to give her – it's all there if you look hard enough, but most people probably don't.

They just see her laugh, wave, call out folks' names with sugar on her tongue – just like she's doing now as she makes her way through the bar, which ain't hard to do since it's about as big as a living and dining room put together. It's the kind of place most people who aren't from the neighborhood stumble upon when they're exploring or because they read on the Internet about how great our fried chicken is. Some walk in and right back out. Some stay, eat and laugh with the regulars and never return.

But it's the people who live around the corner, up the street, and a couple blocks over who keep this place going. They come in every day: their wearied brown faces, their hair gray, their walk slow, carrying loads of weight on their frame, burdens of an unjust world in their step, and tales of their youth they trade like baseball cards – like the exact day they arrived in the big city, or how much their daddy paid for the family's three story row house, or what year all the whites left their street and headed for the suburbs.

But "Ellavators," excuse me, "Ellavators at Petworth," is the last thing from the old neighborhood left on this street. These folks keep coming in here because they went to high school and college together. Raised children on the same block and wept over the ones who got lost to crack. They've fried fish for each other, had rent parties, sat on each other's porches and watched their world change so fast it seems impossible to catch up.

I have Ms. Angie's usual, a Bombay Sapphire gin and tonic, easy on the ice shuga, on the bar before she even sits down.

"Not yet shuga," she says. "I'm singing tonight."

Wednesday is Karaoke night and every Wednesday Ms. Angie comes in and says she's singing. Then she'll say:

"Give me a shot of courage first, Terrance."

And I'll pour her a little something. And then another. And another.

I ain't heard her sing yet and I've been working here over two years.

I just keep pouring her drinks. Night after night. Drink after drink. I try my best to watch out for her. It took me about a year, but I learned how to delicately cut her off before she starts falling off the stool and ending up spread eagle, showing her bright colored panties or worse her privates to the whole bar. If she doesn't stagger, wobble, or trip out the door with one of the regulars or a stranger she meets that night, then I usually call her a cab, put the fare and a little extra something in the Ahmed's hand to ensure she makes it through her front door.

But I also had to learn to keep my distance ever since that night, about three months ago, when she hung around until everyone but Maria and Pedro in the kitchen had gone. I didn't think much of it, figured I would just walk her out like usual, but then while I was cleaning the glasses, she said:

"Oh my, I seem to be the last woman standing. You wouldn't mind taking me home, would you, Terrance?" she asked real cool and easy like.

I didn't want to say yes. But I couldn't say no. So I didn't say anything. I just wiped down the bar one last time and came around to get her.

And then I held Ms. Angie by the elbow and led her outside. But when we got to the doorway she stopped and untied her little jacket from around her waist and brought it to her shoulders. I took one arm and put it in the sleeve and just as I helped her with the other, her little bitty-self reached up and kissed me. And it wasn't no sloppy drunk kiss either. No. It was gentle and intentional, like she had been thinking on it for a while.

At first I thought I was losing my mind, but then when I felt her tongue in my mouth, I damn near smacked the hell outta that old lady. But I also felt kinda weird. Or kinda guilty cause it wasn't all bad. Wasn't all bad at all. And I knew like so many men before me that if I wanted her, then I could have had her, taken her home and released all the good and bad in me - into her. But I took a really good look at her, past those glazed eyes and saw nothing but vacancy there which I imagine hurts worse than pain. So I just pushed her away and took her elbow again, like those 30 seconds had been swept up in a vortex. Before I could open the door, she stopped me.

"You're not gon' tell anybody, are you, Terrance? Please. I couldn't stand it."

I wasn't sure if she meant the ridicule or the rejection, but I just said, "No, Ms. Angie."

And I never did.

"I'm wanting to sing Terrance. I already put my name on the list. You know I used to sing don't you," Ms. Angie asks me now and pushes the drink away.

"Yes, Ms. Angie."

I know what she's going to say before it's even out of her mouth. It was a good story the first time I heard it.

"I used to be what they call a session singer, did back-up for lots of big time artists. You name 'em, I sang with 'em: Stevie, Aretha, the Elements, Luther. But I was good enough to sing lead now. Make no mistake. I was classically trained by the best, Ms. Lucille Winters who didn't just take anybody. Back then she was the only vocal teacher for black folks, so you know she worked with the best," Ms. Angie had shared, my first week on the job. She was about three drinks in. Real drinks, cause I make them strong. It's the only way I know how.

I was new to bartending, hadn't yet learned that 90% of it is listening and keeping your damn mouth shut, so I asked, "Oh really? I like all of those artists. Who was your favorite?"

Ms. Angie dismissed me like I had stopped her on the street for an autograph, then continued with the conversation, that was obviously with herself.

"You know I sang the chorus for Fresh Prince and Jazzy Jeff's *Summertime*? Yep. 1991. I was 30-years-old, living in New York. I got the call from my manager that they needed someone in the next couple hours and would I do it for two grand? And rent was due too? Shheeeiiiit. I was there. And it was the simplest thing to sing, no range, same tone, didn't even get to do any vocal tricks."

I barely got out an, "Oh--"

"Who knew they'd be playing that song, every year, from Memorial to Labor Day, with everyone singing along. And all I got was a measly two thousand dollars? Seemed like so much money back then. And then a little while ago I read an article in *EBONY* magazine or was it *JET* 'cause you know they're pretty much the same...anyway...Jazzy Jeff said he couldn't remember who sang the hook, that it was just some session singer. I almost had the nerve to write in and say, 'Ms. Angelina Worthington isn't just *some* session singer.' But who would believe me," Ms. Angie said as she brought her Bombay and tonic to her lips.

I didn't know any better, it was only my first week in, so I asked the dumbest question ever that everyone in that bar, in that neighborhood already knew.

"You still singing?"

"Honey, no. Haven't sung a song since 1995 when I left New York for good. That world, the music business was no place for a woman like me. I couldn't survive it."

I would come to learn about the "it" from the other customers who spoke about Ms. Angie with lowered voices and side eyes, while she was in the bathroom, or out for a smoke, or leaving on the arm of another man. "It" was New York City; a manager turned husband who beat Ms. Angie then abandoned her and their two daughters; daughters who would eventually turn their backs on their drunk of a mother; a bottle of gin to keep sane; promises from men; and a talent that was good but not good enough, that forced her to come back to her mama's two bedroom apartment and to folks who kept saying to her as they all stood together at the bus stop on their way to menial jobs with minimum wages, "I thought you were going to make it big. Thought we would see your name in lights."

"I'm singing tonight, shuga," Ms. Angie calls out now to Mr. Ray who's sitting in his usual seat at the end of the bar. He's drinking, his usual two fingers of bourbon with three cubes that melted an hour ago, real slow as if he's savoring every swallow and is not just cheap as hell. He holds up his glass, nods, smiles and says:

"For real? I remember you and those girls did that show at the Howard Theatre, 197--"

"Don't even start with the dates Ray. Just say we were looking fine and sounding better."

"Indeed y'all was," Mr. Ray says before he turns his face back towards his glass.

"Sure I can't get you something to take the edge off?" I ask.

"No, honey. I had one of those days where the world tries to knock you down to the ground and keep you there. My little heffa of a manager had the nerve to try to tell me...Well it doesn't matter. It's just...it used to be a time when this would happen and all I'd wanna do is sing – in church, in the club, in a studio, all through my house. Sing until I wasn't sad anymore. Sing until I shined. Haven't felt this way in a long time."

She doesn't look at me when she says this, more looks past me, into her own world where only music is allowed. I can't imagine what could have happened today 'cause seems like in this heat you'd just leave folks alone. But I've never seen her this way, so determined, so present. Wonder if anyone in here has.

Ms. Angie gets real quiet and watches the stage where some girl is stumbling through "I Will Survive."

"Shameful," Ms. Angie mutters.

And then Mr. Williams goes to sing his standard, Marvin Gaye's "Distant Lover" and the whole time Ms. Angie is just sitting there like she don't feel this sticky heat that's clinging to every single body part, with nothing to drink, tapping her long neon pink fingernails on the bar.

The DJ calls, "Mizzz Angelina Worthington is our next performer tonight."

People turn their heads all over the place and mutter to one another, until Ms. Angie rises from her stool and makes her way to the stage. Mrs. Jenkins leans into her husband and says, "Oh he was talking about Peaches?"

Ms. Angie heads towards the stage, but this time her walk is different. Her hips don't swing hard like usual. No, this walk is more deliberate, like a queen approaching her throne.

She takes the microphone from the DJ, brings it to her mouth, and says:

"Testing one, two, testing. Good evening y'all." She smiles but shows no teeth.

And then she stops like she wants to say something else, like she's Diana mothafuckin' Ross and wants to thank her fans for coming tonight. But she turns to the DJ instead. 'You ready?' he mouths. She nods her head. He goes to press the button. She clears her throat. Pause.

And then they just stare at each other, like they're the only two people in the room. And now the whole place is watching them. Everyone stops sipping drinks filled to the top with ice. Side conversations hush. No one moves and you can almost see the heat rising off folks' fingertips. Ms. Angie nods one last time. The DJ presses the button. And she turns to face us.

And then she closes her eyes, tilts her head back, brings it forward, and waits.

The music starts and even though it's Karaoke, the first few notes are still recognizable – a whirlwind of strings and then the voice. Ms. Angie's voice. Round. Smooth as the words to the signature *Porgy and Bess* song unwind like gold silk off a spool.

Summertime and the living is easy.

Somebody hollers out, "Yessss....Lawd."

But Ms. Angie doesn't acknowledge. Doesn't move. With eyes still closed, as the notes dance off the tip of her tongue, her voice lifts the song higher until it hits every corner of the bar and cleans dust out the corners. As the song moves towards the middle, the voice takes the shape of butter dipped in honey poured slowly over Sunday morning biscuits – so delicious and sweet, it's dizzying.

The room goes still and for the first time you can really feel a breeze but no one seems to notice or care. Instead, everyone is holding their breath, enjoying the ride of Ms. Angie's voice, as it loops, dives, *spreads its wings and takes everyone to the sky.* When she gets to the end, she holds that last note so long, it feels like she's going to take all this muggy air with her, swallow it whole, and cool the entire place down.

The music ends and the voice stops just as easily as it began.

And Ms. Angie is gone, off the stage, down the aisle, and out the door, this one time drunk off applause and admiration - a ball of shine and glitter like a shooting star, finding her place in the summer night.

Diana Veiga is from Silver Spring, Maryland and currently resides in Northeast DC. She is a graduate of Spelman College and American University.

GIRL ENGINEER
by Therese Keane

I never thought of myself as a gender barrier breaker, but it happened—twice—before I was 25. In the broadcasting workplace of the early '70s, men groped women and/or sabotaged them if they entered their closed circle of male dominated jobs. Today the Washington, DC airwaves are filled with women hosting television and radio programs, and directing the action behind the scenes in control rooms and out in the field. That picture looked quite different when I came to town 40 years ago.

As a broadcast major at the University of Illinois at Chicago, I hosted and engineered my own show at the campus radio station (mostly playing Joni Mitchell). My job goals after college were not lofty. Major jobs, both off and on the air, were held by men. There were few female role models, and even fewer in the engineering side of the business.

After graduation, I moved to Washington where my sister lived because I thought it might be easier to find a job in a smaller market. My first break was at WTOP-TV (now WUSA) where I toiled for six miserable months buried inside the sales department as a "TWX girl," ripping advertising orders off a TWX— a kind of teletype machine. A TV engineer at the station told me about a vacation relief program at NBC-WRC which hired engineers to fill in during the summer months. The TV slots were gone, but radio had openings. I called the radio station's chief engineer every day for two weeks. When he finally called back, he interviewed me over the phone and hired me. "See you Wednesday, sunshine," he said.

Sunshine? My joy at landing a job at a major DC station and escaping the TWX helped bury negative thoughts about having a letch for a boss. Maybe he's just an old, avuncular type who calls all women "sunshine."

When the elevator doors opened on the radio operations floor, the chief engineer, Harvey Rees, was waiting to greet me. He was in his thirties with a thick brown mustache and a bad toupee. When he saw me, his smile faded and he looked down. His manner turned cold and professional as he showed me the radio operations studios for the Top 40 music and news programs.

He later explained why he was disappointed seeing me for the first time.

"You sounded black over the phone with your low voice and you were from Chicago. I wanted a twofer," he admitted, referring to the affirmative action label for a woman who was also black. Later, I pondered if I was a "one-fer" since I was a white woman, although I had never heard the term. I felt oddly lucky and diminished at the same time.

NBC-WRC Radio had two studio control rooms in 1973. One— the NBC network studio—was usually dark and empty, designed to record occasional news programs or spots by TV reporters. The other—the WRC local studio—was bright and bustling. A DJ sat in a small enclosed booth, giving hand signals to his engineer through the glass window of the control room, signaling him when to start the music, an ad or public service announcement (PSA). Adjacent to the booth and control room was an open editing room where another engineer commandeered a series of waist high, reel-to-reel tape recorders.

Harvey introduced me to the edit room engineer.

"This is Bob, our senior guy here. Bob, this is Therese. She's one of our vacation relief engineers. Bob will show you the ropes."

Bob was more of the avuncular type, a pleasantly cranky engineer, jaded, ready to retire, and fed up with "Brother Love," the morning DJ. Brother Love performed a daily routine talking with a mouse that acted as his radio sidekick. He managed this by having Bob record in advance Brother's voice for the mouse's side of the conversation. Brother gave Bob a tiny metal tube to fit over the capstan on the tape machine which changed the playback speed so Brother's recorded voice would mimic one of Alvin's singing chipmunks, which apparently is what a mouse sounds like when it talks. At a designated time each morning, Brother Love would signal Bob to play back the mouse's part of the conversation.

Bob often reminisced about Ed Walker and Willard Scott, "The Joy Boys" whose program he had engineered years earlier. They were replaced by the jock format.

"Now those guys were a class act, not like these jerks," I had not heard the Walker and Scott show, but somehow felt that no one could replace them in Bob's ears. I was 23 and I really liked the current Top 40 music format, but I'd never admit that to Bob.

"Well, I think it'll be a good experience for me to work here," I responded, "I'm kind of excited about working in live radio." Bob rolled his eyes in despair.

During the summer, I filled in for the DJ board engineers when they took their vacations. The pace was fast but I kept up once I got the rhythm of the predictable format. I glued my eyes on the waving hand signals of each DJ to know when to push the button for the next music, commercial or mouse conversation. One time I misunderstood one of Brother's extraneous hand waves and pushed the button for an ad while he was still talking.

"She socked me in the mouth with Preparation H!" He shouted angrily off-air. "I want that girl engineer off my show!" Brother Love was neither brotherly nor loving, but he had clout as a highly rated morning DJ. I was removed and banished to the darker news editing studio to help less excitable network reporters record their sound bites. At first I was devastated by being bounced from the board, but it provided a break from the tedious music format, hearing the same songs in rotation over an eight-hour period.

Brother Love had little tolerance for mistakes by girl engineers but he wasn't as dangerous as the afternoon jock, Bobby, who looked like he wore a carrot colored toupee. I found out one day—the hard way—that his hair was real. While I was bent over an editing machine, he quietly emerged from his booth. There was no one else around. He quietly wrapped his arms around my midsection from behind, pulling me against him. I yelled at him to let go, but he wouldn't. I tried to wriggle free but he tightened his grip. I stretched my arms up and back and managed to reach his hair which I pulled as hard as I could.

"Ouch. Why did you do that? You messed up my hair!" He screamed.

"Oh, yuck! It's caked with hair spray!" I gave him the most disgusted look I could muster, which wasn't difficult since my fingers were stuck together from the residue. I noticed with satisfaction that several orange hairs were sticking straight up, making him look like a drunken over-the-hill rock star.

In 1973, it never occurred to me to complain about what today would be a blatant sexual offense. I was afraid of getting fired. Since Brother bounced me for a mistake caused by his careless signal—and no one defended me—I assumed my complaint would be disregarded. Sexual harassment cases were rare at that time. I did, however, tell all the women throughout the building about Bobby's sprayed hair and Neanderthal advances. Word spread quickly through the female ranks. They ridiculed his vanity and imagined what might have happened if I had actually pulled off a wig!

Bobby never touched me again.

My vacation relief job ended with a young DJ who was still unknown but would later become famous. He was a lanky kid, with a surfer tan and sandy hair brushing across his eyes. He called himself "The Greaseman." His normal voice was surprisingly light for radio and he exhibited an "aw shucks" personality. But when he went on the air, he dropped his voice into a sinister bass register and contorted his face menacingly. He dubbed me Elvira, his silent sidekick. Off the air, I'd tell him what I was doing socially and chose my stories carefully since they sometimes ended up in his routine.

"Elvira went to the ballet last night and saw lots of twisting and twirling," he growled into the microphone, making the ballet sound like a sadistic horror show. During his off-air breaks, he reverted back to his sweet persona and shared his stash of mini Snickers bars with me. He was married and I had a boyfriend so our relationship was strictly platonic. But his Jekyll/Hyde persona was a bit creepy and I never really understood it.

One evening during the Greaseman show my Chicago parents came to visit. My father was horrified at the dingy subterranean atmosphere of the windowless studios, and concerned that I was the only woman working among a crew of sloppily dressed guys that he eyed warily. The Greaseman's radio voice didn't help his paternal concerns.

"Why couldn't you have gotten a nice job as a secretary? Why are you working in this awful place?" he asked.

"But Dad, I'm the first girl engineer they've had here! It's a big deal for me, and I'm getting paid a lot more than a secretary would." My father, unconvinced, wandered around making sure the engineers knew he was checking them out.

During an off-air break, my mother and the Greaseman found each other. He was flashing his million dollar white smile, pushing hair back from his forehead. She was totally charmed. My mother had four girls and no sons, so she relished every opportunity to mother a potential foster son.

"Therese, you work with some very nice young men. And the fact that you're the first woman to do this job—well that's really great. I'm so proud of you!"

I returned to the control room and she watched me through the glass window. Her smile faded a bit as she heard her charming boy turn into the Greaseman, with his growl and twisted face. I waved at her reassuringly as she was leaving.

Mom waved back. She had a mini Snickers bar in her hand.

Another girl engineer, Marianne, was hired midway through the summer. She was pretty but had no experience in broadcasting and botched one of the DJ shows very badly. Harvey had left the station and was replaced by a new chief engineer unfamiliar with my abilities. After Marianne's debacle, he made the unbelievable announcement: "No more girl engineers on the board." He never gave a reason why I was banished. Aside from socking Brother with Prep H, my board work had been excellent. I was reluctant to defend myself because my summer relief position was coming to an end. I had my "first girl engineer at WRC" title with experience at a big station and didn't want to cause trouble in my final days. I was looking forward to moving on, hopefully to that production slot I was still dreaming about.

During the next four months, I found no production jobs in TV or radio. Then in February 1974, I heard about a full time radio engineering position with the Mutual Broadcasting System. Broke, I reluctantly applied and was immediately hired. Again, I was the first woman hired as a radio engineer at that old venerable network. There were no DJs, just news anchormen and reporters. The job consisted of cutting sound bites with editors, running the board for live newscasts, and taping news conferences and congressional hearings in the field.

When I entered the Mutual editing room on my first day, the engineer I was relieving silently got up and walked out. I looked at the editor—a woman. She didn't appear surprised that I had been deserted—only mildly annoyed.

"We've got a feed coming in from the Pentagon. Plug in four rows down on the panel on your right. Start rolling tape on deck three."

I quickly found the Pentagon line, plugged in the cable, and rolled the tape. Her directions were perfect.

"I'm Annette. Welcome to Mutual. Don't worry. I know what you need to do. I'm just not allowed to push the buttons because of union rules. When we get a break, we'll get another engineer in to help you," she assured me as she turned to answer a phone.

But no other engineers came in to help. Their lack of concern made me feel they were hoping I'd fail. Annette, who was the first woman editor at Mutual, trained me for the edit room operations. The other engineers ignored me.

Some engineers spent most of their time in the field assigned to the White House, Capitol Hill or the Pentagon. Danny, a short middle aged man who sounded like a mobster, spent his days on Capitol Hill. At the end of his shift, he'd return to the bureau. When he first saw me he fell silent, and walked away. I was now adjusting to this reaction. Whenever he was required to speak to me, he called me "the girl engineer."

Annette warned me: "Don't take your eyes off him. He sneaks up from behind, squeezes your tits." I was not shocked since I'd already beaten off the lecherous Bobby at WRC, and wondered if these guys all belonged to the "attack from behind" club.

Eventually I was assigned to assist Danny on the Hill. We were sending a live feed back to the bureau from a Senate hearing with Henry Kissinger. Danny asked me to pick up some coffee and donuts from the cafeteria. I did not see this as sexist. I was the junior kid who did grunt work for the senior engineer. Besides, I was starving. When I attempted to enter the hearing room with the donuts, an iron arm shot out barring my access with a mild karate chop to my rib cage, upsetting my tray. I watched in horror as the donuts flew onto the floor, one heading toward Kissinger, who continued in his accented drone, turning briefly to monitor the path of the pastry.

"Stop, let her in, she's the girl engineer. She's with me!" Danny ran toward the Secret Service agent who dropped his arm as Danny approached.

Clearly annoyed, Danny asked me, "Where are your tags?" referring to the chained stack of photo IDs the press wears around its neck to access Washington's halls of power.

"I put them in my pocket. They were getting stuck in the donuts," I responded sheepishly. I could see that Danny wanted to drag me by my ear back to the bureau.

"Never, never take off your IDs, understand?" Danny helped me retrieve the donuts as I pulled the IDs from my pocket and replaced them around my neck. Kissinger was still droning on, unperturbed.

Despite this incident, I felt encouraged. Danny had acknowledged, "She's with me" part of his team. I happily dusted off my donut and bit down.

My official acceptance to the ranks of network engineers happened at the White House. In the Nixon era, women were not allowed to wear pants, not even pant suits, inside the White House. Men were required to wear suits and ties. I always wore jeans to the bureau since much of the work entailed crawling around dirty floors, plugging in cables. There was a regular engineer assigned to the White House so it was unlikely I'd be working there.

One morning I arrived to learn, due to a staff shortage, I was assigned as the pool audio tech for a news conference with Father William McLaughlin who was supporting President Nixon's reelection. That priest later became the TV commentator, Bill McLaughlin. Mutual had done an FBI clearance for me the previous night. When I arrived at the White House, there was an outcry from the other engineers, sweating in their suits. Not only were they allowing a woman to do the pool—she was wearing jeans.

As the pool tech, I was the only engineer allowed inside the room once the conference started. The others sat outside in the hallway with their cables plugged into my audio feed. If I blew it, none of the networks would have sound for their newscasts. This was my first pool audio. I was terrified.

The news conference began. I rode the audio, adjusting the volume up and down between the reporters and the priest making sure I wasn't too slow to bring up the audio, or too fast bringing it down thereby missing parts of questions or answers. My palms sweated, my shoulders were hunched over. I moved nothing except my hands for 45 minutes.

When it was over, I felt exhausted, stiff, and parched. The suited engineers were removing their plugs from my feed. They got to their feet. I checked the location of the Secret Service agents for help if I was attacked by a cable swinging mob.

"One of the best feeds we've ever gotten." They were smiling. "Great job, Therese!" Obviously, they had forgotten my old name: Girl Engineer.

Therese Keane's essays have appeared in the Washington Post *and the anthology,* The Pen Is Mightier than the Broom. *She produced and hosted radio interview programs for the Smithsonian Institution and for WETA-FM, including the award-winning "Conversations from the Kennedy Center" and "Women of Achievement." Therese lives in Penn Quarter.*

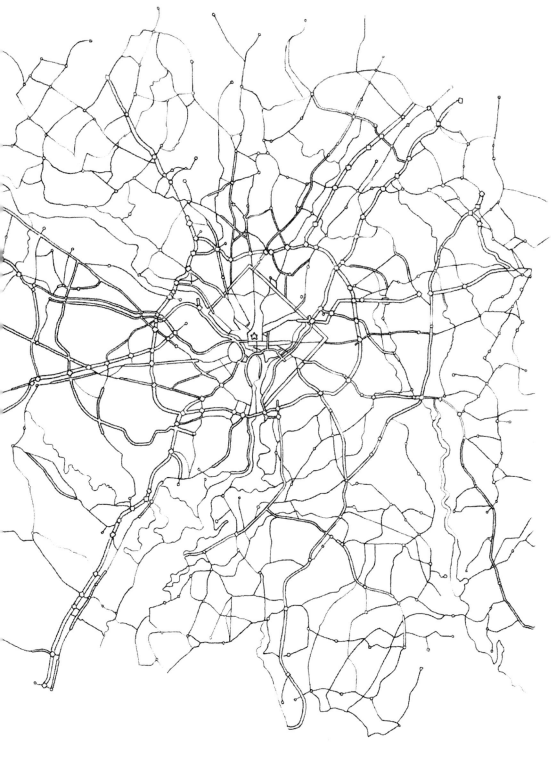

Remembrance.

DAVID KIRBY IN MY HEAD
by Edna Small

I'm at the refreshment table at the Library of Congress
        having just heard a poetry reading by David Kirby
and Li-Young Lee, a poet whose work I have loved ever since
        a suitor sent me a copy of *From Blossoms* when we were
first courting and he thought the sensuality would speak to me,
        which it did, but he did not; it seemed a prior girlfriend
had sent it to him, but I am grateful to him for the introduction
        to these poems and feel like I have been at a feast tonight

not only for the delicious sounds – and sight – of Li-Young Lee
        who is really gorgeous with dark hair and such deep eyes,
but also for the extensive narratives related with much humor
        and ultimately sly wisdom by David Kirby, a poet
whose work I did not know but found fascinating to listen to.
        So I am spearing asparagus into the creamy dip
and picking up skewers of broiled salmon that can be dipped

into soy sauce and chatting with my friend Patsy about the virtues
        of freecycling at the same time that I am watching the line
of readers clutching newly purchased books and inching
        their way to Li-Young Lee's signing table where
an efficient member of the staff is asking people's names
        and writing them down for the poet, which not only helps to get
the spelling right but also saves his voice, which was strained
        this evening, as he had such a bad cold but he persevered

as Patsy does in asking me about freecycling –
        she seems more interested in free food and how to get
free goods than in the poetry. Actually she's here
        mainly to get a ride home as she works nearby and lives

99

on my block and I don't mind as I really don't like walking
       to the car by myself so I tell her about how I gave away
twelve lectures on existentialism from *The Teaching Company*

that I got as a 2-fer when I requested a series of lectures
       on the history of the English language, that I may actually
listen to in my car, which, like me, is old enough
       to have a tape player, yet I know I will never
listen to tapes on existentialism – I have enough trouble
       with the meaning of poems in the *New Yorker* – so I offer
them on freecycle and get two responses, but not one
       complete sentence. Not that I mind run-on sentences

but one said only, "I need to expand my metal horizons…
       write me if it's free," leaving me a picture of metal
stretched by the idea that freecycle items, are, indeed
       free. I have a strong preference to respond to requests
when I'm not tempted to correct the spelling or content
       unless the writer is not a native English speaker,
in which case I often feel great admiration especially

as I can hardly speak a clear and direct sentence
       in any of the foreign languages I've studied and studied
but have not learned. In my late twenties, I was in Mexico
       and bought a set of dishes in an open market and wanted
to ask for something to ship them in, armed with a Spanish
       phrase-book and 4 years of high-school Latin, including
the year in which our fourth year Latin teacher, Miss Popper,
       who lived with Miss Bales, always called on Billy Goldstein

to translate the purple passages as his cheeks were slowly
       suffused with blush; Billy and I were the only two juniors
in a class full of seniors who snickered when Billy stammered
       and also seemed to share some knowledge of our teacher's private
life that was outside the realm of my limited knowledge, so now

I tried to improvise, after asking *donde puedo encontrar*
I made up a word for "carton," and met the same kind of snickers

as Billy had, and only later when I took a course
    did I realize I had asked for *cojones*, balls, which
in a way is what I had making up words like that.
    Finally the line has dwindled, and I tell Li-Young Lee
how much I like his poems, and ask him if he would sign
    the books I brought with me, and he is gracious and inscribes,
"Fellow flower, let's keep opening," in his book entitled
    Rose, and it's not until later that I make the connection

and Patsy asks me about the other response to my offer
    of tapes, and I tell her the second, *"I'll take it. Where?"* was even
worse and less related to anything; but I have had time
    to reflect that we all do our best to be understood and don't
always make the right connections so I gave the tapes to the guy
    who didn't proofread and was not sure what to believe but knew
that he, like all of us, needed some metal exercise.

Edna Small *is a retired psychologist living and writing in DC. She is a member of the Federal Poets and Poets on the Fringe. Her poems have appeared in* Beltway, Federal Poet, *and* Prospectus.

THE THINGS WE CARRY WHEN WE COME FROM SOMEPLACE ELSE
by Faye Moskowitz

"Hoarder" is the fashionable word to use now for people who can't let go of things. You know, the kind of folks you read about in the *Post* Metro Section, recluses who die alone in homes where newspapers, stacked to the ceilings, form aisles so narrow it's almost impossible to remove the body. There's always a line about how many dumpster loads it took to empty the place. I worry lately about who will clean up after me when I am gone. There are days when a sash cord breaks or the play room ceiling leaks again, and we swear to make good on our vow to find a little condo in the Kennedy Warren, before it's too late, two bedrooms, maybe, instead of the seven we have now.

David Shlomo, my maternal grandfather, lived to be 107. He roomed with us for years when I was growing up in Detroit, a natty little man with a trim white beard and a nicotine-stained mustache. Striped garters held up his white-on-white shirt sleeves, and he wore a tall black yarmulke when he was in the house, more to cover his bald spot than for religious reasons, we all suspected. I remember him reading the *Forward* with his round glasses perched slightly askew on top of his head, the skull cap pitched crazily toward the back. Zaideh was a minimalist; he knew only two phrases in English: "Pack o' Luckies" and "Same to you." That seemed to take care of his needs out in the *goyische* world and among his non-Yiddish speaking grandchildren.

Zaideh was a hoarder. Sometimes he sat at his bedroom window so he could see to sew the few dollars his children gave him into his union suit. Hidden near his doorway, I watched the needle go in and out of the thick material, the glasses on his forehead catching the morning light. Inevitably, wash days were a problem. He and my mother argued bitterly about that underwear. "Gott mit dir, Tateh,"

102

my mother would cry. "What will people say? Let me have that union suit!" She sent my poor brother to fish the underwear out of the bathroom on the infrequent occasions when Grandpa could be persuaded to take a bath. "Gevalt!" Grandpa would shout. "They have robbed me; the gonifs have robbed me."

This will be my 82nd summer, 50 years of living in Cleveland Park. I don't wish for my Zaideh's age, and I don't consider myself a hoarder; collector is so much more benign a word. But here I am, alternatively dreaming about "sheltering in place," and worrying about how long I can continue to hike it up the stairs to the third floor. In any case, I don't know what to do with all I have accumulated. Some time ago, I went to an "estate sale" of a neighbor who had died weeks before. To my credit, I felt a bit unsettled about strangers pawing over her possessions, the things for which her children had no use. Her clothes hung on padded hangers in her closet, hats long out of fashion stored on a shelf above, and fine leather shoes, size five, sitting in shoe trees below. I bought a slim beige evening bag made of "genuine reptile." When I got the bag home I opened it, and in a zippered compartment found two dollar bills and some loose change. The purse still smelled faintly of her scent, something familiar, Chanel perhaps. When had she last carried that purse? To a gala at the Kennedy Center? A diplomatic reception? For what eventuality had she thought to bring along the bit of money? She seemed so alive to me at that moment, and I feel so alive today, just a bit out of sorts at the intimations of mortality this focus on divesting brings.

"The world is certainly a sudden place," says Frankie in *Member of the Wedding.*" More and more I know what that means. The results of one blood test can turn that world around. One misstep on the stairs and the nursing home looms. Not to sound overly dramatic, but actuarial tables don't lie; numbers brook no arguments. I'm determined to get a handle on all this while I still have the energy to do it, set out gamely one morning, green trash bag in hand. This is my mantra: one bag at a time. I can do that. Anyone can do that. But it's only 9:30 AM, and already I'm in trouble. Here is a portfolio of crumbling kindergarten drawings, some from Michigan, some from John Eaton School here in D.C. A name in block letters stumbles across the bottom of each: Shoshana, Frank, Seth, Elizabeth. Underneath the pile of "vanilla" paper artwork lie paintings on wrinkled newsprint, slashes of green grass, naïve blue skies and dripping suns like teary yellow eyes. What to do? Only a total stranger could trash them, or the archives of pale green paper on which penciled ABCs struggle to learn the discipline of wide-ruled lines. I stuff the papers back in the envelope. Let the stranger deal with it.

Upstairs in the cedar closet, more decisions. What about the dozens of imprinted yarmulkes commemorating long ago bar and bat mitzvahs or weddings, or the stuffed animals without which this grandchild or that couldn't fall asleep when they spent the night here? How can I part with the *peltz*, the storm coat with sheepskin lining, the one my husband was wearing when he met me, the one we brought from Michigan all those years ago in case it ever really got cold in Washington, the one that's never left the storage closet? Last Thanksgiving Frank was stunned when I suggested he take back to Columbus some of the games he had played with as a child. "Don't tell me you and Dad are planning to move," he said, as reluctant for things to change as I am.

When I think of hoarding, I conjure up a pantry in our house in Jackson, Michigan. And when I think of that pantry, I see stacks of tall cans filled with Premier Brand corn on the cob. There must have been an overstock that my parents picked up somewhere in the panic about WW2 food shortages. I don't recall that canned corn on the cob was a particular family favorite, one my mother feared would blight our growing up if we were deprived of it. In fact, we had the best of all corn worlds right at home in Michigan: fresh ears tucked in their moist pale green husks and sweet smelling silk, plump kernels bursting milky juice when you poked one with your fingernail. All summer, farmers hawked the corn from wagons that rolled up and down our street, their wares only an hour or two from the fields. Perhaps Joan Mondale remembered similar Minnesota summers when she formed a co-op in Cleveland Park years ago, so she and our neighbors could enjoy fresh produce from local farmers.

Some fellow Democrats from Michigan had already made the move to jobs with the new Kennedy administration, and Cleveland Park was a popular destination in the early '60s. The rambling Victorians, mostly as yet unrestored, were perfectly suited to the four children we all seemed to have produced. The pioneers lauded the proximity of the stunning Washington Cathedral, still under construction and John Eaton Elementary, a viable grade school for families familiar with fine public schools back home. (We learned about private school options soon enough.) Many of the younger children learned to swim in the Cleveland Park Pool which was slightly larger than our claw foot bath tubs, but a welcome oasis from non-air-conditioned homes for exhausted mothers during the afternoon "Adult Swim." "Passing the test," a neighborhood rite of passage, meant swimmers could go to the pool without adult supervision.

For the most part, mothers stayed at home. In summer, the children played in the quiet streets, disappearing in the morning, grabbing a quick lunch and then disappearing again, only to come in for supper when we summoned them by African drum, cow bell, bugle, or xylophone, each child recognizing the family signal. We sat with them while they ate; ready to serve a late warmed-up dinner to the men when they finally dropped their brief cases in the front halls, sometimes after the kids were already in bed. The neighborhood boasted congressional and senatorial staff directors, assistant secretaries of this and that, state department officials, Foreign Service folk on home leave, newspapermen and lots of lawyers, all of them convinced that extra hour in the office would change the world.

We could walk to Wisconsin Avenue for shopping. Our staples came from the Newark Street Giant, specialty items from Charles of Capitol Hill, all supplemented with treats from the University Bake Shop. Once the kids were old enough to traverse 34th Street, every mother's secret nightmare, the kids could vanish into Murphy's Dime Store where the Candy Lady dourly weighed out the carefully pondered treats, picking one off the scale or adding it for perfect fairness. In later years, a pet shop in Murphy's basement offered a few sad looking rabbits, some lethargic guinea pigs, and always, before a clerk could remove it, a gold fish floating, bleached belly up, in the murky fish tank. At the Zebra Room, we scarfed pizza, still relatively exotic, noted Rep. Carl Albert at the bar, and tried vainly to keep our adolescent boys from the notorious graffiti-covered walls and the condom dispensers near the downstairs toilets. Egg salad sandwiches and Cokes drew us to Peoples Drug's lunch counter, Chinese food to the Moon Palace, and in McLean Gardens, a Hot Shoppes was reserved for a special lunch to celebrate a birthday or even a time to commiserate with a child who was feeling outnumbered by overbearing siblings or suddenly treacherous friends. "Cross at Macomb," we said when we let a child go off to Wisconsin Avenue alone. "Cross at the Light!"

Connecticut Avenue offered a potpourri of international cuisine: Pouget's for French food, Roma for Italian, Yenching Palace, said to be frequented by Henry Kissinger, for people-watching. But the kids would have eschewed any of them for fried chicken at Howie's Chick'n Bucket near the firehouse. And God bless Mr. Rose, wherever he is. Rose Jewelers acquired heirlooms from Foreign Service widows in apartments along the Avenue. An entire collection of English ironstone, a set of Tiffany flatware, a fully equipped ship's bar: with each purchase, I bought into a stranger's past.

Those long-ago children and grandchildren have gone on to pass tests far more significant than the one at the Cleveland Park Pool. So what am I doing, nattering, the green garbage bag still empty? Jack and I have few family heirlooms to pass on to our family. The things our parents and grandparents carried with them in the move from the shtetl to America were at once elemental and ultimately obsolete. Bobeh Raisel's featherbeds filled with down from her own ducks gave way to conventional mattresses soon enough. When I knew her, Jack's Bobeh Freda had put her marriage wig away in mothballs in favor of a print kerchief bound around her head and tied at the back; she looked like a wizened Halloween pirate. Her brass candlesticks will go to our granddaughter, Helen. (Such a pang as I write this; perhaps she will light them on Shabbat more often than I have.) I do have the mantel clock, salvaged from my father's junkyard. It marked off the interminable hours at family seders; most of us children were asleep under the table or lying cross-wise on Bobeh's bed well before we got to the gefilte fish.

For years, my mother kept in a cedar chest, a heavy coil of brown hair the barber gave her soon after she landed on Ellis Island and opted for a modish bob. I wonder who came upon the wrinkled paper bag when she died. Seeing its contents glistening with naphthalene and curled around itself like a small animal, did they drop it in a trash can, faintly disgusted? My mother did put together a set of dishes after the War, the Red Apple design from Franciscan Ware. The dishes came, a few at a time from California, and we certainly never used them, except on Pesach. Other than some translucent cups and saucers from brief trips to Canada, my mother was no collector like me. My father was forever grumbling that she stood over him while he read the *Citizen Patriot* at night, impatient to snatch it from him so she could wrap the supper scraps in it or use it to sop up the water on her freshly scrubbed kitchen floor.

In 1960, I was elected a Stevenson delegate to the Democratic National Convention that eventually nominated JFK. At 30, I was one of the younger delegates and as a woman, one of the few minorities. All of it was new to me: golden California, home of the Red Apple dishes; the venerable Biltmore Hotel, the sense that I was a small part of making history. Mostly I hung out with the Stevenson staff who, having relatively little money, eschewed the glitz of better-funded candidates and held court in a kitchen off one of the main ballrooms. Their prize was Eleanor Roosevelt, sitting on a simple wooden stool, greeting delegates. I still remember how she looked in her flowered dress and brown velvet toque, and how despite her diminished size, her presence dwarfed the room. Somewhere in the thousands of political and cause buttons, I've collected since, is the Stevenson Shoe, a silvery stud with the famous hole in the sole. If the empty green trash bag doesn't spell trouble enough, I'm tempted to sift through those buttons now, just to make sure I haven't misplaced it.

Recently, my former next door neighbor who had moved to Florida wrote me of how successfully she was downsizing. "I have some old political buttons I'm trying to get rid of," she told me. "You can have them if you're still collecting." Why didn't I tell her I was trying to simplify my life also? Why didn't I suggest she sell the buttons on e-Bay? Why didn't I describe the dilemma of the green trash bag? When the buttons arrived, crammed in an old candy box, I spent an entire morning sorting them. JFK, LBJ, McGovern, McCarthy, Humphrey, Gore. I could have constructed my D.C. life from those buttons.

The Cold War was still raging when we moved to Cleveland Park; the Cuban Missile crisis posed a moral dilemma before we had unpacked the moving boxes. What to do with the Quakers down the block who refused to consider the bomb shelters we were exhorted to build. The head of Civil Defense lived on 34th Street. Surely he had a shelter. At dinner parties, we sipped our cocktails and debated whether or not to let the Quaker parents and their seven children into the shelters most of us never ended up constructing anyway. Instead, we sent our kids off to John Eaton where they practiced "Duck and Cover" as protection against "The Bomb" or a missile, and we were blissfully ignorant that their teacher led them in The Lord's Prayer every morning.

We've been in this house so long, the night sounds peculiar to it are as familiar to me as Jack's gentle breathing or the unintelligible dream conversations he carries on as he lies alongside me. From time to time, the stairs sigh as if under a heavy weight, and the foundation creaks in response. Then the memories come, bidden or not. I think of the beautifully designed drafting table that Seth, not yet old enough to drive, discovered late one night set out for the trash men in a Georgetown alley. "Mom," he whispered at my bedroom door. "You've got to help me get it home." And so, at 2:00 a.m., I slipped shoes onto my bare feet, covered my nightgown with a trench coat and grabbed my car keys. It's not given to every mother to become a hero in her son's eyes so easily, but I did that night. The table was indeed lovely, a wide sloping surface of pale birch set on legs as slender as the reeds we call cattails. Seth took it to college and in some subsequent move or other he had to leave it behind. The table is as clear to me as the night I saw its blonde wood shimmering under a floodlight in that Georgetown alley, and yes, I regret its loss as I regret so many things I can no longer account for.

An old Yiddish saying teaches that when a man or woman dies, a library is lost. As I go about my sifting, sorting, deciding and discarding, I remember Grace Paley's wisdom: "It's always about the story." When people move on they make choices about the things they carry and what must be left behind, as my parents did when they came to America. Fortunately, they carried their libraries in their hearts, no baggage limit; books of their faith in God and in The Promised Land, books of family love.

I have inherited my family's libraries. All along, I realize, I have been passing those books down to my children, just as they came to me. And I have been accumulating my own library, stories of Red Apple dishes and Stevenson Shoes. The tale of the drafting table is a volume in my library, and my son has a copy. The good news is that these books take up no visible space, they are all first editions, they are easily transported, and their value increases each time they change hands.

Faye Moskowitz, a professor of English and Creative Writing at George Washington University, is the author of works including A Leak in the Heart, Peace in the House, *and* And the Bridge is Love, *recently republished by Feminist Press.*

RETURNING
by Rose Caryn Levine

Every night, like clockwork, my father arrived home at 5:25 and dinner was promptly served at 5:30. I was never on board with this schedule. I was the first of my friends who had to be home for dinner. I always had to leave early, just when I thought all the fun was beginning. Most people ate at 6:30, but the Leonards up the street didn't eat until 8:00. This was fodder for the gossip mill. Did Allen really work that late? Was he having an affair? Worse yet, out drinking? No wonder their sons were so sickly. Who ever heard of children eating so late?

By 6:15 the kitchen had been wiped clean and the dishwasher set in motion. The entire evening still loomed ahead. During the school year it was time for homework and maybe a TV show before bed. My brother and I didn't always agree on what to watch, but we both loved *I Dream of Jeannie* and *Lost in Space*. Would Jeannie ever escape from the bottle after Major Nelson had corked her in yet again? Would the Robinson family ever find their way back to earth? These were ponderous questions we took quite seriously.

In the summer we would head outside to play. We lived on a cul-de-sac jam-packed with kids who all tumbled out after dinner. Since we ate so early my brother and I were often the first ones out and had to amuse ourselves until the others finished their meals. We each had glass jars with air holes drilled into the lid. We filled them with grass and twigs, then trapped caterpillars with the hope of seeing them weave cocoons and turn into butterflies. I remember one happy occasion when my caterpillar miraculously morphed into a moth. I watched breathlessly as I unscrewed the lid and it flitted away.

We played kickball almost every night. The older, bossier kids always declared themselves captains and took turns choosing teams. As one of the younger children, and a girl to boot, I was often chosen last. This hurt my feelings but I tried hard not to let it show. Once I started crying when some of the older boys didn't want me to play with them. Ashamed of my tears, I ran inside to hide. My mother wouldn't let up until I told her what was wrong. She then threatened to go outside and make the boys play with me. I begged her not to, but she wouldn't listen. She strode right out the front door and into the street. The game was suspended while she made a scene and my position reluctantly reinstated. I couldn't risk that sort of humiliation again. Thereafter, I kept a stiff upper lip while waiting for my name to finally be called.

The bottom of the cul-de-sac, right in front of the sewer, was home plate. Many baseballs had been lost down the drain. One of the braver boys would pry open the sewer lid and shimmy down to retrieve them. After a while kickball became the game of choice simply because the ball was too big to meet such a demise. The tree in front of my house was first base and second had been painted in white directly onto the street. Third was the crack in the driveway across the street. If the pitcher missed the ball, it was possible to run to all three bases and make it back to the sewer without being tagged. This was especially exciting when the bases were loaded.

My family ate dinner quickly with little conversation, barely coming up for air. You would think we didn't know where our next meal was coming from. I learned early on that if you ate too slowly there was no hope for seconds. Every few days or so, though, my mother would lay down her fork. I recoiled, knowing what was coming next. She'd stop chewing and a smile would cross her face. "I know what we can do tonight," she'd say. "Let's go returning." That line made my skin crawl. Returning seemed like a punishment to me. It meant no TV, no kickball. My brother, by virtue of his sex, never had to return. This was strictly women's work.

My mother loved to shop, but couldn't bear to try clothes on in the store. I don't know if there is a psychological term for this affliction. Dressing room phobia? If she wanted a new blouse, she would buy four, take them all home, then try them on in her bedroom. Sometimes she would keep one, sometimes two, other times none. All the rejects were immediately stashed into their respective bags and carried to the trunk of her car as if, once rejected, she could no longer bear to look at them. They would languish there for days until the inspiration to return struck.

In the early '70s, downtown Silver Spring was a sleepy, dying town. Montgomery Mall had recently been built in Bethesda and that's where most serious shoppers did their business. When it first opened, I remember going there with my parents to see what all the fuss was about. "This is just a craze," my mother said. "People won't like it. It will never last."

Up the block from the AFI Silver Theater, where City Place now stands, was the Hecht's department store. Next door was the Woolworth's 5 &10 which, with all its baubles and trinkets, was an endless source of fun and entertainment. It also contained a lunch counter, but I never saw anyone actually eat there. There was a jar of pink eggs near the deep fryer that had been there for years. It was intriguing, yet frightening, a science experiment gone wrong. If my father was with us (he sometimes came to shop, never to return) we would sit on the swivel chairs and order Cokes. My father swore that fountain Cokes were better than the ones you could buy in the grocery store, and I hold that opinion to this day. One of the greatest things was an inside door connecting Hecht's to Woolworth's. You could go between stores without having to step outside. That way parents could shop (or return) at Hecht's while their kids ran around Woolworth's without having to worry about them going into the street and being run over.

When it was a night to return, my mother and I would drive to Silver Spring and haul the rejects out of the trunk. We'd walk quickly and purposefully from the parking garage to Hecht's, a woman and a girl on a mission. There were usually three or four people ahead of us in line waiting to make their purchases while we waited to return. My mother would fidget for a minute or two, scan the room, then say, "Wait here. I want to look at something." My job was to stay put and hold her place in line. Child abductions were unheard of in those days. Hecht's was a safe place. There was no traffic inside, therefore no need to keep an eye on your child. Off my mother went, eying yet another blouse destined to be returned.

I grew impatient waiting in line. The longer I stood, the more time my mother had to select her doomed purchases. I'd think longingly about the kickball game and wonder who was winning. I even went so far as to think a trip upstairs to the children's department might be fun. I'd wince if the overly-chatty saleslady made small talk with her customers. That only gave my mother more time. When it was finally my mother's turn to conduct her return transaction, she often took the opportunity to teach me a lesson or two about finance. She advised me to always pay for things with cash. That way you knew exactly how much money you had to spend. If you made a habit of charging your purchases, you would lose track of things and be unpleasantly surprised at the end of the month. There was one exception to this rule, however. Clothes must always be paid for with credit. That made them much easier to return. If you paid for your clothes with cash, you would have to go all the way to the business office on the third floor and obtain a special receipt before you could get your money back. If you charged your clothes, no questions were asked. With one magic swipe your credit card was simply reimbursed.

As a teenager my friends loved to spend Saturday afternoons at the mall. My mother's prediction never came true. Montgomery Mall was a thriving shopping Mecca and teen hangout. My friends seldom bought anything. They just liked to look around, then maybe get a snack at the food court and check out cute guys. If they found something they really liked, they would put it on hold, then go home and whine until their mothers broke down and bought it for them. I usually didn't accompany my friends to the mall. I found it kind of spooky. Once in a while I came reluctantly because I had nothing better to do. The prospect of a cute guy sighting held some appeal, but I found no pleasure in recreational shopping. I still don't. All those nights of returning left me traumatized. I don't think there is a name for that disorder, either. Post-traumatic-return-disorder? PTRD? Today if I absolutely need to buy something, I drag myself to the store, hone in on that item, and make a bee line for the exit.

I recently discovered online shopping. I was late to the game, but now I'm hooked. What a pleasure it is to shop from the comfort of your own home. When your package arrives, you can take it into your bedroom and try the clothes on. You can keep some items, return others. You can even return all of them if you want. Your package arrives with its own ready-to-affix return label. You can make your purchases disappear with a quick trip past the UPS box. You can log onto your computer at any time of day or night and look around for more.

I think my mother would approve.

Rose Caryn Levine *grew up in Silver Spring, Maryland and currently lives in Washington, DC. A voracious reader, she has worked at Politics & Prose for the past twelve years.*

ELSEWHERE
by Chloe Yelena Miller

*I don't want to talk about it, for fear of making literature out of it
(...) although as a matter of fact literature originates within these
truths.*

- Mourning Diary by Roland Barthes

The Potomac River floods

   when it rains

      elsewhere.

I slept in the next room

   as you were dying.

      Elsewhere.

Dying.

   Gerunds and

      their continuous action.

Would have died.

   The conditional engaged

     with the past.

Mourning.

    Morning.

     Unmooring.

"(Mourning)

   Not Continuous,

     but Immobile."

Where are we after the dying?
                      My heartbeat
                                shatters thought

like the soprano,
                      eyes blank
                                singing over the hospice bed.

 "No sooner has she departed
                      than the world
                                deafens me with its *continuance."*

Now.
                      Then.
                                At the time.

I start at the beginning.
                      Simple past tense
                                happened.

I carry the book to the river.
                      Key Bridge stretches
                                into a short horizon.

Water, traffic, wind rush.
                      Keep breathing.
                                Sometimes a gasp.

Listen. Smell. Feel.
                      But. "I no longer hear.
                                Like a localized deafness…"

Listen:
                      Birds, helicopters,

                    chest rattle.

I follow paths in Rock Creek Park.
          Walk on the pipe-path,
               unleashed dogs growl.

Elsewhere.
          Without a heaven.
               You lodge in our hearts.

A fish rib
          in my throat at dinner.
               Quicken the pace.

Heart beats,
          exertion.
               Faster.

At your hospice bed,
          air mattress breathing
               in regular time.

I gasp.
          Will you
               to breathe

with me.
          "Suffering like a stone …
               (around my neck, deep inside m

The covers laid,
          legs and hip turned.
               Passive voice, body.

After,

I return home,
                    "confront the long series of times

without her."
                    Elsewhere,
                                    the bed, the river, your voice lock.

"I know now
                    that my mourning will be *chaotic*."

I sit in the dark room,
                    wanting to read.
                                    Birds, helicopters above.

"Does being able to live
                    without someone (…)
                                    mean you loved her less"?

Home, I'm lodged too far away.
                    Both of us
                                    installed elsewhere.

Lodge.
                    The present tense.
                                    Active.

                    Elsewhere.

*Poet and essayist **Chloe Yelena Miller** teaches writing privately, at Fairleigh Dickinson University and at Politics & Prose Bookstore in Washington, D.C. Her first poetry collection,* Unrest, *is available from Finishing Line Press.*

A KNOWN PATSY
by Glen Finland

Maybe you remember him. Could be he gave you a quarter once, too.

For five years in the late 1970s I shared a brick wall with the custodian of our three-story Capitol Hill apartment building. I had the sunny ground floor garden apartment that looked out onto a busy sidewalk. The old custodian lived behind me in a windowless room that shook from the eternal spinning of washer-dryers lining the hallway. I ate take-out from restaurants along Pennsylvania Avenue. He ate cat food out of cans.

A small man with a Chaplinesque walk, a child's smile, and large arthritic hands, Alex Bogardy was the one whose door you'd knock on when your sink backed up. The one you'd call to come clean up the unexplained vomit left on the front stoop after someone else's long night out. If you asked him how he was doing, even right then, he would counter with a chuckle that revealed a graveyard of broken teeth. "Couldn't be better," he'd tell you, and then he'd reach into his pants pocket and drop a quarter into the palm of your hand. Not just yours, but anyone who asked, and he'd do it every time. To most of the Hill's panhandlers, Alex Bogardy was a known patsy.

He was also a painter, a boxer, an inventor, a castanet-playing Gypsy and a Catholic who never missed his daily walk to Mass.

Alex enjoyed his nightly drink at the VFW Post next door to us on the corner of Third and D, SE. He drank Bull's Blood, his own concoction of orange juice and strong red wine from his native Budapest. He never told me how old he was, but two or three drinks always sent him down to the floor of the bar for a set of 25 push-ups to keep himself "in fighting trim."

He said he'd studied the castanets at the Peabody Conservatory in Baltimore and for years had accompanied Flamenco dancers around town. He showed me photos of himself performing at a Bethesda goulash restaurant. With his castanets held high in the air, he wore a bolero jacket and high-heeled black boots, his head tilted in deep concentration under a fringed gaucho hat. At night I heard him practicing through our shared wall. From time to time he would invite me over for a little show.

The room's bare concrete floor offered top acoustics for Alex's castanet playing and fancy footwork. He claimed as a young featherweight boxer in Baltimore he had been knocked out cold a few too many times, and that the percussive force of the shell-shaped clackers kept his broken-down fighter's hands nimble enough to paint.

Beside a messy cot pushed up under his sink, his castanets sat on a wooden table next to his record player and his cache of LPs in their dust jackets. And next to them—his easel, crowded with tubes of oil paint and natural brushes of all sizes. Dozens of his original paintings covered the room's four walls. Most portrayed Jesus surrounded by lambs, angels with perfectly coiffed hairdos, and frequently a tumescent Adam and a large-breasted Eve, naked in a flowery garden that was home to a waterfall, dinosaurs, and a coiled snake. Bible verses written in Alex's careful calligraphy started at the top left of many of the paintings and continued on down the side and back around to where they had begun, so that you had to crane your neck this way then that way to follow the whole thing through to the end. One of these Adam and Eve paintings he insisted I take for my apartment. I have it still, hanging on a nail somewhere up in my attic.

The ceiling of Alex's little room was trimmed with the cast-off hubcaps he collected along Pennsylvania Avenue or sometimes pilfered from expensive cars parked behind the Library of Congress and the Supreme Court. These he accented with glitter, ribbons and the essential biblical quotations, or sometimes with priestly types whose engorged penises stuck out of their long dark robes. Taken all together, the big penises and full breasts in his artwork never came off as porn, but rather as the artist's simple salute to humanity.

I had always been curious about the mauve tint of Alex's thinning hair. Some weeks it was brighter than others. One evening I came home from a weekend away to find he'd left at my door a copy of his paperback, The Secret Art of Hair Coloring. He told me he'd self-published it after his patent for a rather pink-looking hair color potion had been accepted by a cosmetic company. I walked out my back door and down the hall to his room to thank him for the thoughtful gift.

His door stood wide open and the lights were on inside. I knocked but got no response and turned to go. Then I heard a moan. It was Alex, crumpled like a broken doll on the floor under his cot. His castanets and several half-eaten cans of cat food lay scattered about the room. Sometime over the weekend he'd taken a hard fall, twisted his leg badly and suffered an unforgiving knock to the head. Dehydrated and disoriented, he was semi-conscious by the time I found him.

The EMTs arrived in short order and bundled him off to an emergency room. But with no health insurance, an insignificant bank account, and no known next of kin, he went from being a daily quirky presence along the bustle of Pennsylvania Avenue to one of those marginalized faces in the crowd that are easily forgotten. In the months that followed, Alex ended up losing a leg to an infection that had set in sometime after his transfer to St. Elizabeth's, which soon enough became his permanent home.

I visited him there a few times, until it was clear he no longer recognized me, and the nurses had become suspicious of my motives. They were legally bound not to pass on any of his personal information to me, a stranger who had walked in off the street asking to see him. I fell into the habit of reading the obits in the Post, thinking maybe that this was a way to keep up with him. But nothing ever came of it.

Thirty years later, I Googled his name on a whim. I found him right away. A link appeared showing a vibrant painting of a well-coiffed naked couple beside a stream. Underneath was this:

Garden of Eden, Oil on canvas, 20th Century American Folk Artist
Alexander Bogardy
Born: Hungary 1901. Died: Washington, DC 1992.
Alex's painting, one of the many that used to hang over his sink
behind our shared brick wall, had found a permanent home. It's there
for all time in the Smithsonian American Art Museum, 3rd Floor, of
the Luce Foundation Center.
http://americanart.si.edu/collections/search/artwork/?id=36505
Maybe we'll remember him now.

Glen Finland *is the author of* Next Stop *(Putnam), a Barnes &
Noble Discover Great New Writers Pick, about the summer she
taught her autistic son to ride the DC Metro—solo—and how in the
process, he taught her to let him go. A freelance writer, she received
her MFA from American University and once worked at P&P for a
brief stint as a math-challenged bookseller.*

Welcome to Historic Anacostia Sign
Photograph by John Muller

1200 Block of Maple View in Historic Anacostia
Photograph by John Muller

John Muller *is a local journalist and historian whose latest book is* Frederick Douglass in Washington, D.C.: The Lion of Anacostia. *A former reporter for the* Washington Times, *he is a current contributor to* Capital Community News, Greater Greater Washington, *and other Washington, DC, area media.*

MIGRATORY FEVER
by Alexandra Smyth

I am lost amid
buildings that appear
like mushrooms
after a dark, humid night.
And I, for the life of me,
cannot remember the last time
I drew a breath of fresh air,
or felt the sun
sprinkling freckles like
cinnamon cancer
across my buttercream face.

This fugue has lasted
a whole damned New York winter,
and now for spring
my body screams
for dogwoods,
pink and white puckers
floating against the green sky
of a Virginia backyard.

I remember
the state routes of veins
on the backs of my mother's hands,
those veins I know will
one day brand my own hands
with middle age,
as she set out the watermelon print jug
for sun tea.

The squawk box chatter
of my fellow apartment dwellers
is starting to
pick pick pick
at my last nerve,
and I find myself
cursing the naked man
in the window across from mine
who so proudly displays
his bait and tackle every morning
as though
I were a wall-eyed
large-mouth bass to catch.

And what to make
of the Catalpa tree that blooms
white and vulgar by the fire escape,
displaying her sizable assets,
while the concrete below her
has so little to invest in?
It's okay,
I whisper to the steadfast gray,
her flowers will fall,
her tits will sag,
you are constant
and unchanging,
a more faithful partner than she.

Though my feet may trod me East and West,
I can only resist
for so long the southward magnetic pull
on the iron in my blood,
and I cannot ignore
the way my cheeks flush
every April,

not unlike the pink
blossoms around the Tidal Basin,
the womb that held me
for eighteen gilded summers.

Alexandra Smyth is a native of the DC suburbs. She is currently pursuing a master's degree in Poetry at the City College of New York. Her work has previously appeared in The Smoking Poet, Specter Magazine, *and* Word Riot, *among others.*

BENT
by David Rowell

It started with the tree.

On our drive home from work each night, Leah and I had been watching a Christmas tree lot that had sprung up on Georgia Avenue, where a used car lot had been. Out front someone had fastened a crudely painted sign to a post that read, "Natural Only, No Pesticides." There were rarely more than two or three people looking around. The lighting was dim. Night after night the trees remained in their spots, like a group of picketers. And yet out of some feeling we couldn't quite name—it wasn't pity, I know that now—we decided this was where we'd buy our tree.

That night, about two weeks before Christmas, business had picked up a little at the lot. There was a man in surgical scrubs underneath his coat and an older couple—the man was using a walker, and his wife held absently onto the bar, as if she might lose him otherwise. There was a heavyset woman in sweatpants and a sweatshirt that showed two reindeer talking in a cartoon bubble that I couldn't read. Someone's kids were running up and down the rows, shrieking and clutching Big Bird and Cookie Monster toys.

We walked uncertainly through the lot, as if we were at a party of strangers. Most of the trees were slumped over, wallflowers. Others had no discernible shape, and still others had so much space between limbs, you could read the brightly lit signs across the highway through them: "dark meat special, 21 pcs." "At Mattress King Size Matters."

"I'm still not done with your shopping," Leah said. "I'm waiting on something that hasn't come in yet."

"Well, don't worry if it doesn't," I said. "I'll still be here after the holidays." I had gotten Leah some perfume and a book on making jewelry, but I couldn't be sure what she'd think. Last year she had taken back the dress I got her.

We walked through the neat lines, humming parts of the same song, when a kid in a ski cap picked up our trail. He worked there and wanted to answer any questions we had. He told us that the trees had come from the western part of Maryland, and we nodded as if that was reassuring to us.

"Were they dragged all that way?" I whispered to Leah.

Every once in a while he'd say, "That's a nice one there," and we'd stop and look out of politeness. He couldn't have been more than 15—he might have had braces—but he seemed to know plenty about Christmas trees. In fact, he seemed to be running the place. The two other guys who were working there were old enough to be his father. They kept coming to him for a consultation.

"What's the price on the seven-footers again?"

"Dave," they said, "do we just have the one kind of stand?"

"Dave, this fellow wants us to knock off ten bucks because of the bald spots."

Did I mention this was when Leah was trying to get pregnant?

"So what kind of tree are you folks looking for?" Dave wanted to know. He said *folks*.

"The triangular kind," Leah said. Dave wasn't sure how to take that.

"Let me show you some over here," he said, and as we followed we noticed the older man and woman studying a tree that one of the workers was holding up for inspection. Their faces were twisted. Dave reached into a line of taller trees and pulled out one that didn't look half bad, only it was curved up top.

"It's kind of bent," I said. Leah's eyes were starting to glaze over. She was getting the twitch.

"We need greenery too," Leah said. This was news to me, and I wondered if she didn't say it out of that nervous habit she has. When she feels stuck with silence she says anything. Our little apartment didn't even have a mantle or even stairs.

"Did you want this one?" Dave asked, and spun the tree for us. The way his eyes washed over it, the tree might have been his homely sister that he was trying to get someone to take to a dance.

Leah said, "That looks like a good one to me."

"What about the curve up top?" I said.

Leah shrugged, and that was that.

She had hoped she'd be pregnant by Christmas, just as she had hoped last year and the year before.

Dave could see I wasn't convinced about this tree, but he waved his hand to one of the older fellows and told him we were going to take it. "Greenery," Dave said.

He walked us over to the clear spot in front of the trailer set up as the little office. A battered space heater was on the ground, and the blast from it felt good on our knees. In the blinking lights over the trailer door I could see Dave had a scar under his eye. It was jagged, as if he had been in an accident, or even stabbed. He reached down and picked through a tangled mound of greenery.

"Not that much," Leah said. "Just eight feet or so."

"Where are we going to put that?" I asked Leah.

Dave said, "If you have a front porch."

"Huh," I said. "Sure." All we had was a doormat.

When he was through measuring off a piece, he pulled out a little calculator and ran the total. It was expensive, and we were just getting by week to week. I told Dave we were going to have a hard time fitting the root of the tree in our little stand, so he got the guy with the hearing aid to bring over the chain saw. Dave watched him intently, his smooth jaw clenched tight.

"Careful, not too high," Dave called out, and the guy stopped for a moment to reconsider. "Careful."

When the man was done he hoisted it on his shoulders, then took a few wobbly steps, as if he were pretending to be drunk. "Which car?" he said.

As we were pulling out, I noticed that the lot had emptied out again. One of the men was crouched in front of the space heater, and the guy with the hearing aid had his hat off, scratching his head. Dave had gathered up one of the smaller trees in his arms, and he was doing something with it, but at first I couldn't tell what. It was an awful-looking tree, with practically no branches on the bottom half. The top half was full and looked like it belonged to another tree. He was pulling at the branches up top so they wouldn't be so bunched up, trying to make the tree more presentable, I figured.

"Dave and his misfit trees," I said to Leah, as we waited for the traffic to break and head home. "Dave's Christmas trees of horror."

"Well, I like the one we have," Leah said.

"It's a little curved up top, but I like it," I said. "I think it's fine."

The traffic on the Beltway was heavy, but we were content listening to Ella Fitzgerald. Leah sang along with "Jingle Bells," her arm tucked under mine. *"I'm just crazy about horse-**ES**."*

Leah said, "What do you think of Ella for a baby's name?" I told her I liked it, though I wasn't so sure.

As we got close to our apartment, we gazed at the big candy canes hooked around the street lights downtown. They weren't much to look at, really—the white of the canes had become yellow with age, and the bows were a bit mangled, but suddenly, with the warm air in the car and Leah leaning her head on my shoulder, I was starting to feel like we were on the verge of better days. I stared at the candy canes and told myself they were beautiful. I wanted to believe.

When we got home we untied the tree and brought it inside. As I pulled it through the doorway a pile of pine needles snaked a path.

"It's leaving a trail so Dave can find it," Leah said. I meant to laugh, but I was busy trying to maneuver it into the stand we'd set out. After tightening the bolts, I backed away until I could see if it was straight. I put the Nat King Cole on, and Leah got the vacuum out. In the light the tree's shape was worse than I had realized. That spot up top was still bothering me, but I didn't see a way that I could cut it and have it look any better. I got on my stomach and eased a pitcher of water below the lowest limb and poured. The draft from our broken deck door was cold against my cheeks.

Outside two fire trucks roared past, their red lights twirling off our walls like frightened birds. In the apartment above us, the sports fanatics were watching a basketball game and apparently unhappy about how it was unfolding. Every time the other team scored, which seemed often, they jumped up and stomped, causing everything we owned to shake.

"God, I wish they'd move out," Leah said.

"I wish *we'd* move out," I said.

"That would be better," Leah said. "When is that going to happen, again?" I smiled, but I didn't have the answer. Neither of us did. Things needed to be worked out first. Two months ago my boss at the garage had told me he was giving me a raise, but then the next paycheck came, and the next, and nothing was different. I hadn't worked up the nerve to ask him about it. Leah's hours at the pet store had been scaled back because business was slow, but she didn't know if she was ready to go get another job just yet. She liked it there. It seemed to make her feel good to say maybe she should go back to school and study to be a veterinarian.

We had our nest of lights out and our box of ornaments, but it was getting late, and the energy we had earlier had dropped off us. We said we'd finish it the next night. There was time.

We didn't know—how could we have ever known—what was about to happen and what it would do to us.

We got undressed and got into bed, though we weren't quite ready to sleep. Leah turned on her side and slid her hand slowly under the sheets, her soft fingers taking hold of me. She said, "Hey Dave, how much for this one here?"

"We can call it an even 60," I said.

"That's a good looking tree," Leah said.

"Careful," I said. "Careful."

David Rowell's debut novel, The Train of Small Mercies, *was published by Putnam in 2011. He is an editor at* The Washington Post *and lives in Silver Spring.*

A LITTLE ROCK AND ROLL AND A GOOD CIGAR
by Patricia Aiken O'Neill

As a teenager in Washington in the 1960s, life was a continuum punctuated by "befores" and "afters" . . . the promise of a vibrant young presidency, then the permanence of its tragedy; the consistency of everyday life across the city jarred by race riots in the aftermath of Martin Luther King's assassination, leaving the landscape, and its people, scarred.

My time in college was a "before" too, as I went from an all-girls school (Stone Ridge, in Bethesda) to Trinity, in Washington DC, an all-girls college. The "after" was to come, less than a decade later. When Georgetown accepted girls, its academic standing rose. Trinity had been ahead of Georgetown, and this now reversed, as the upper middle class Catholic girls who formerly had populated Trinity instead flocked to Georgetown.

Trinity was across town from where we lived and each day my father dropped me off on his way to work. It was an island in the midst of a changing landscape and getting there was an introduction to a diorama foreign to me. Although the land had not yet been razed by the 1968 riots, the geography of the housing was different and the living was more obvious: row houses (no "townhomes" then) almost to the curb, with big front porches that seemed to be the focal point of communal living. The combined themes of loud music and laughter added local color and signaled vibrancy that our northwest neighborhood lacked.

Our neighborhood, our family, had been quiet since my sister's death two years before. In the 1960s no one talked of death, particularly the death of a young person. Death was private, to be borne alone; the Washington area supported two daily newspapers then, and neither reported the cause of death. It was like reading a story that skipped the final chapter. I wonder now about the guilt that must have encased Mother and Daddy's wrenching grief – that they couldn't stop the steady advance of Death that stalked Paula for the six months of her illness. Of course, they and the doctors did everything that was possible then, but afterwards, the feelings of failure wouldn't stop their relentless review of Paula's life as she grew and, unbeknown to us all, the disease inside her grew accordingly, as identical as a twin. One time I watched Mother examine a photo of Paula as a teenager. Her eyes mirrored wonder and confusion. She was looking for a physical outward manifestation of the internal blot on her daughter's short life. Paula was beautiful; there were no signs to see.

So, there was a separateness to our time together in the car each morning. Daddy would seek solace, drawing on his beloved cigar, and I, to combat the nausea of the fumes emanating from the morning smoke, would turn to the AM radio, stopping on whichever station was playing a Beatles song. "Listen," sang Paul, my favorite, "Do you want to know a secret?" (dum de dum); my mood would lighten as my focus shifted and my upper body gyrated with the rhythm.

"Do you promise not to tell?" continued Paul. I became as lost in thought as Daddy appeared, as he was soothed by the heady aroma created by the cigar. The cacophony of sound freshened the stale air, absorbing the smell which by now surrounded me. Laced with smoke, it created a weave of patchwork which alternated with the blue sky just outside our windows. Then, my school's dome appeared, peaking above the architecture surrounding it, adding an exclamation point to its neighborhood.

I welcomed the chance to lose my identity as my dead sister's sister. At the same time, I relived the trauma, and couldn't help but repeat the horrors that I had witnessed in her dying process to a rapt audience of girls just introduced to me. Years later, studying for my masters in social work at Catholic University, still repeating the same route to get across town, I realized that the repetition was a form of therapy, helping me move beyond it when I ran out of words. As horror does, the retelling eventually lost its impact as the well of tears always ready to surface lessened to a trickle.

Trinity expanded my world, so constricted by Paula's death. I found joy in my history courses, my new friends, the possibilities that college promised. That brought a new assertiveness and I decided to approach Daddy about my objections to the early morning cigar smoke. Daddy was formidable, projecting an elan and surety that could easily be beyond my reach. So I practiced, copying Daddy's negotiating skills and approached the subject in the car one morning. The Beatles were absent from the radio that day and there were spaces to fill.

It took more than one try. The first time my communication dissolved into typical teenage angst, ending on a note of self righteousness and indignation. I quickly dissembled and lost the point. The next time was more successful. Daddy was an avid listener, and even better, a doer who found solutions, but first he shared that my music was too loud. He suggested a solution for each of us: he would open the driver's side window – cars manufactured in the 1960s featured an extra triangular shaped section in front that opened up – directing the smoke towards it and flicking the cigar's ashes out of the car; I would lower the volume on my rock and roll music. The outside sounds would balance the inside decibels and neutralize the air.

Each of us was content. Daddy began to listen to the songs and not just react to the sounds. He looked forward to certain favorites and when they played would tap his feet in a snappy rhythm to the beat, thump the steering wheel with his hand – the one not holding the cigar – and smile broadly. He became part of the decade. I tolerated the cigars, appreciated his effort, and held my breath (keeping my counsel).

Our arrangement lasted for as long as we shared the car each morning. By senior year, I was driving my own car to school – an early graduation gift. Perhaps Daddy wanted to smoke his cigars in peace.

Not too many years later, Daddy died. His cigar cutter, a beautiful, curved piece of carved bone tipped by the requisite steel blade, remained untouched on the coffee table. The car ashtray became a repository for toll-way change. The absence of smoke precluded any reminder of my feelings toward cigars…for a while.

Gradually over the years, my antipathy towards cigars dissipated like the smoke that had stifled me. As the air cleared, I began to understand the ritual that was as crucial as the smoke: the importance of stroking the cigar, smelling it to inhale its freshness, the expectation, capped by the climactic inhale and exhale. In my young experience, I had trivialized it. It was Daddy's anchor each morning, starting his day, like others start with coffee.

Only recently have cigars entered my life again, at first to a surprising welcome. The odor no longer overwhelms me, as it's become the aroma of a positive time lost to me long ago, quickening my senses and stirring fond memories. I become expectant as the smoke holds my attention, mesmerizing me, setting the stage of my personal séance and revealing a moment in time. Someone else may hold the cigar, but in my mind's eye I see my father in the plumes, stoking it, savoring it, flashing it in his jaunty manner. His head is uplifted in a salute to the good life. He is in the driver's seat, tapping his foot in time to the music – my music. I smile knowingly, feeling that the only thing separating me from Daddy is a good cigar.

Patricia Aiken O'Neill has lived in the Washington DC area since she moved here as a young child when her father joined the Truman Administration. She is a graduate of all local schools, up through and including law school. She recently retired from her position as CEO and president of a national health care association, with headquarters in Washington DC. Her personal essays and professional articles have been published.

GRANDMOM MOVES TO ALASKA
by Janice Lynch Schuster

She longs for trees and night
Both left behind for the land
Of midnight sun. She had not expected
To live out a century on the cusp of America.
Born in the nation's capital
This place so foreign to her.
She misses the long walks from Brentwood
To shops on H Street, she misses
Her childhood, her brother, the bed
They shared in the crowded living room.
She remembers the wind, the day
A tornado ripped Bladensburg
And she and Billy huddled in a ditch
While fences blew skyward above them.
Here she is so far from her own life.
Loneliness has carved a space
Beside her, and behind. She prays
And sometimes God whispers in her ear.
Memories fill her time. There is little else
Except a corner for her crossword puzzle
And her books. Her great-grandchildren,
15 of them, congregate in her thoughts.
She cannot keep them straight.
She is bent 90 degrees to the ground
Which one day will take her old bones
And heart and send them home.

Janice Lynch Schuster, a native Marylander, has published poetry and essays in many journals and newspapers, including Poet Lore and the Washington Post. She writes about aging and health care for Altarum Institute.

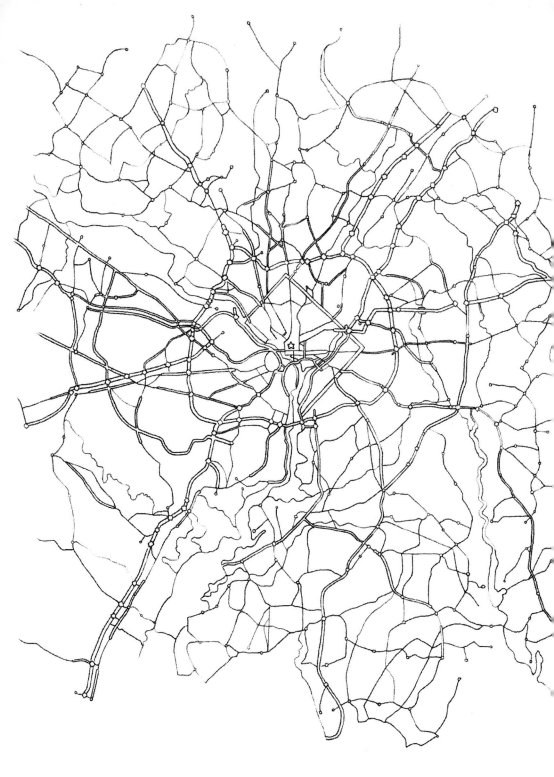

Transience.

ONE-TENTH OF THE BODY
by Sandra Beasley

The ship's steward didn't know what
he had photographed.

They looked at that smear
along the berg's base, red paint
from the Titanic's hull—

and called it
        the wound,

as if the North Atlantic's ice
had gashed its side in sympathy.

But they had seen only
one-tenth of the frozen body.

What they thought a shroud
no more than
        a kerchief,

the red silk any disaster
tucks in its pocket
before stepping out to dance.

If a metro car comes behind another
and mounts it,

that first squeal sounds
almost like
        joy.

On the Red Line train, a man
watches the floor peel away
beneath his feet.

He knows what happens
when you set tinned fish free.

Sandra Beasley *is the author of* Don't Kill the Birthday Girl: Tales
from an Allergic Life *(Crown), a memoir and cultural history of food
allergies, as well as two poetry collections*: I Was the Jukebox *(W.
W. Norton), winner of the 2009 Barnard Women Poets Prize selected
by Joy Harjo, and* Theories of Falling *(New Issues), which won the
2007 New Issues Poetry Prize. She lives in Washington, DC, where
she serves on the board of* The Writer's Center.

CHICKEN BONES
by Jacquelyn Bengfort

Chicken bones. You move to Bloomingdale in February, fresh off a ten-month deployment and freshly out of the Navy, all dewy-eyed over the chance to start your dream writing career in the biggest city you've ever had a chance to live in, and you find yourself often as not staring at the pavement. Usually your Staffordshire bull terrier finds them first anyway, a convincing testament to the power of the canine sensory suite. They—the bones—are ubiquitous, though you've never seen anyone eating chicken (or anything) on the street, and you're out at all different times of day. (You did once see a small flock of songbirds fighting over one of the bones—quite unsettling to your pescatarian sensibilities, and stomach.) You were always taught as a kid that poultry bones are bad for dogs, so each walk becomes a desperate battle to keep the dog away from the delicious detritus besmirching the sidewalks and alleys of the neighborhood.

You walk, alone this time, pet-less, to the Metro station in Shaw. Sometimes it's lovely, sometimes there's someone behind an open second story window, exuberantly playing an upright piano and everything smells like hothouse flowers. But sometimes you're walking back home looking over your shoulder because you just filed your first police report on the guy who tricked you out of 20 dollars while you were sitting on the platform (note to con men: as a mark, a woman who grew up working class on the Great Plains is gullible but not stupid—she knows exactly how many 20s are in her wallet). Sometimes you're cutting across LeDroit Park, five months pregnant and walking faster than some people jog because some guy is following you (note to players: no one is named "girl," it's been years since she could be called a "baby," and she's probably not being "nonchalant.")

You try to start a poetry-based webcomic about living in the District. You promise yourself, "Self, we're doing this. Twice a week, indefinitely." Then twice a week, 50 installments. Then 13. You make it to 12 after four months. Still not done. Though you may have touched greatness with the piece about the possum-versus-dog battle in your backyard. You find that you don't know enough; not about the city, not about the next block. If there's a vibe, you're a broken bit of catgut, not vibrating.

So you focus on your work, the writing, sending off short stories with hope and being debilitated with each rejection. Five blocks away, in Eckington, your brother-in-law is also trying to be a writer. You don't call him, though, or much talk about it when you see him. For fear that things are going just as badly for him. Or, worse— much, much better. Like when you went to that reading at Big Bear and everyone was so obviously so much better than you. Dedicated, and brave, and (that grail of grails) published. You find some freelance work that pays, a little. You're grateful your husband's job comes with health insurance. You start planning meals so you can be sure to afford the mortgage. This isn't how you expected your dream writing career to feel.

Bloomingdale is not the core of the problem. Bloomingdale is lovely. Everyone says so. This is the core: you don't know how one makes friends once all grown up and out of school and working out of the home or staying at home eating ice cream and waiting for inspiration with a capital "I" to come along. There are no coworkers at Your Home & Co., LLC to go out with for drinks at closing, no classmates to debate with in your third floor office that is really more grandiose than you deserve. When you catch a glimpse of the Washington monument amongst the turrets of the neighborhood, will you feel lucky? Awestruck? Or guilty that you spent two hours at lunchtime re-watching old episodes of "The Office" and being jealous of their scripted camaraderie?

All you hear about Bloomingdale is how friendly it is. That and how it floods every time it rains. You have material proof of the latter in your basement in-law suite, currently under renovation. But the first bit—sometimes you're not sure. It probably didn't seem too friendly to the group of pedestrians held up at gunpoint on your block this past spring. Or maybe you should just stop reading the *Post's* crime report each Thursday, and picking out the good bits to email to other family members in the area. (By good, you of course mean a combination of "worst" and "nearest our homes.") Maybe you should sacrifice an evening to a civic association meeting. Or use your fascination with petty crime to head up the neighborhood watch.

You hope your incipient child will be a good excuse to meet the neighbors. Everyone likes both babies and hearing themselves give their very best advice, and you know how to be polite no matter how unwelcome that advice might be. You have military training and impeccable manners. It's a tradeoff you'd be happy to make, listening to unwanted counsel regarding pacifiers and infant sunblock, if it meant an acquaintance.

So you walk in Bloomingdale, sometimes alone, sometimes with your pet, soon enough with your baby, and you see neighbors talking to neighbors and you wonder when you'll be a part of it, how to make that happen. How to be not just a watcher and walker—not just a failing writer with a beautiful desk—not just another young pregnant woman and her dog, staring at the concrete, looking out for chicken bones.

Jacquelyn Bengfort spent 18 years reading library books and staring out at the North Dakota prairies before departing for stranger shores. Her writing has appeared in The Labyrinth *and* Storm Cellar *and at the 2013 Baltimore Playwrights Festival. A graduate of the Naval Academy and the University of Oxford, she lives in Washington, DC with her husband, her daughter, and a dog named Winston.*

ODE TO THE DUPONT CIRCLE METRO ESCALATOR
by Deborah Hefferon

Your bounty of corrugated treads rolls by my tentative feet. I choose
the next one offered - you lift me. Your handrail races by, I grab hold.
My eyes are drawn up to a swatch of blue; I daydream on the ride.
Emerging from your womb, you carry me into being. Streetscapes
greet me: half smokes with onions, bargain folding umbrellas, bouquets
of baby's breath, a dapper man singing gospel, his bowl full of dollar bills.

You're fickle. This day you are still.
Awed by your stagnant grade, humbled
by your incline, dizzied by your distance,
I begin my journey without your help. Tempted
by false confidence, I shift left, sprinting past gaspers,
eying my strappy shoes. As my heart quickens, I slow down,
dare to glance up. My, you've grown! Forced to surrender right,
I curse your stubbornness, your refusal to give me a lift. A hitchhiker,
abandoned, doomed and damned to scale you forever, until my chest explodes.
A homeless man at street level offers his hand as I crawl up the final riser. I grab hold.

*Deborah Hefferon is an independent consultant working in the fields
of international education and cross-cultural training. Her personal
essays have appeared in* The Pen is Mightier than the Broom,
NAFSA International Educator, The Christian Science Monitor, Iris:
A Journal About Women, *and* Potomac Review. *She loves living
within walking distance of Politics & Prose.*

145

WHISPERS FROM THE CAPITAL BELTWAY
by Nathan Blanchard

On the outer loop of the Capital Beltway I-495, by Exit 33 (MD 185/Connecticut Ave) the highway whispers. It does not figuratively whisper: it literally whispers. Other beltway exit ramps never whisper. Most citizens used to know and talk about it. In fact, the whispering road was a national celebrity for several decades.

In 1957, Exit 33 was part of a two-mile-long section of what was then called the Washington National Pike. President Eisenhower's Federal Highway Act incorporated the road into the beltway and the four lane highway was widened into six lanes between 1957 and 1959. The Governor of Maryland in 1959, J. Millard Tawes, accelerated work on the Capital Beltway, scheduling its completion for 1964. A journal written by a construction contractor documented his experience at the site. Arthur Combs, born 1932 in Chevy Chase, MD, wrote on May 8, 1960:

> When I am near [Connecticut] avenue, having spent all day in the blistering heat of the sun, I hear murmurs. They are faint, but they are no less disturbing. I turn toward the sound and there is no one. I am frightened still now, in my recollections.

Reports of drivers hearing a voice began sprouting up not long after the beltway was completed in 1965. Early testimonies of drivers who heard the voice described it as a gravelly male baritone devoid of regional accent who whispered or murmured encouraging and inspiring proverbs. At first, single words and sentence fragments were all people could discern because the traffic noise of motor engines and wind obfuscated the whispers.

"From little acorns, mighty oaks do grow" was the first full quote transcribed by Dorothy McDougal, who scribbled the proverb on the back of a grocery receipt while she maneuvered the wheel. *The*

Washington Post picked up the story, and she was interviewed for a feature article. People began transcribing as much as they could, and once the story ran in the November 13, 1966, Sunday edition of *The Washington Post*, people began sending in their quotes.

The Washington Post opened a column in March, 1967, called *What's the Road Saying to You?* Readers were encouraged to send in their name, age and occupation, along with what the road said to them. The road tended toward quotes apropos of the time of day or the season. For example, during the flu season of 1971, the road whispered, "Feed a cold, starve a fever." For six weeks in 1974, the road whispered to early morning travelers, "You cannot unscramble eggs." Every Sunday from 1973 to 1979, it said, "Practice what you preach." This made most of the public believe the road was Christian, and in 1980 the road was baptized by the First Baptist Church of Bethesda, MD. Between 1965 and 1979, the road whispered thousands of sayings and catch phrases. Among them are:

"Pride is said to be the last vice the good man gets clear of."
"One good turn deserves another."
"You have to kiss a lot of toads before you find a handsome prince."
"Calm weather in June, sets the corn in tune."
"Don't judge a book by its cover."
"Don't cry over spilt milk."

People in the late 1970s began debating the party affiliation of the voice. Republicans claimed the voice's support by quoting it saying, "Necessity never made a good bargain." But Democrats made their own claims when the road said, "he that lives on hope will die fasting." The jury remains out.

In the early 1980s, bumper stickers and T-shirts featuring the road flooded department stores and catalogs. "Wishes won't wash dishes" showed up scribed on planks hung above kitchen sinks nationwide. Traditional American idioms and proverbs began to be attributed to the road.

People began to huddle on the edges of the off-ramp, trying to hear the voice, but only automobile drivers heard the voice. Radicals congregated under the I-495 overpass on Connecticut Avenue for weeks at a time. Montgomery County Police routinely broke up groups and demonstrations. In the mid-1980s, the voice became more frantic. For all of 1984, it only said, "You don't need a weatherman to know which way the wind blows." When Bob Dylan was interrogated about his knowledge of the road, he dismissed his implication by saying "I don't even remember writing that line."

Not everyone was privy to the spectral murmurs. The whispers came randomly, and could not be predicted. A survey conducted by the Maryland Motor Vehicle Association estimated the average number of whispers at around 4,000 a year. Witnesses varied in all demographics. No common denominator could be established to help predict or explain the phenomenon.

The town of Kensington, which is located just north of Exit 33, became a tourist spot for people visiting the road. Merchants with whispering road paraphernalia lined the shops. They sold key chains, trinkets and keepsakes, all featuring the road's sayings or a colorful illustration of a highway.

At the 1986 MTV Video Music Awards, Billy Gibbons of ZZ Top wore a t-shirt displaying an image of the Exit 33 road sign. Columbia Records attempted to record an album of the road, but no voice could be heard on the tapes, and the project was shelved.

In 1972, the beltway was extended to eight lanes, but it wasn't until the 1990s that Maryland widened the four miles from I-495 Exit 31 north to Exit 35 (I-270) in Bethesda. The early 1990s saw the first commercial slogans repeated by the road. "Maybe she's born with it. Maybe it's Maybelline," was the first. The L'Oreal Group refused to comment on the endorsement. The road would only whisper slogans once they had penetrated the culture's psyche. Throughout the 1990s, "Just do it" was the most cited commercial slogan whispered by the road.

The late 1990s chronicled a decline in the road's activity. Reports petered out to fewer than five a month. The last column of *What's the*

Road Saying to You? ran on September 10, 1999. It contained two submissions of the same quote: "Close, but no cigar."

From January 2001 to November 2008, the road did not speak. Only a gentle weeping could be heard from time to time. Media coverage of the road dropped. Public opinion slid the road into marginal conspiracy theory mumbo jumbo. When it finally began to speak again, it was too soft for most people to hear.

It's odd that such a paranormal experience, validated by so many people, could vanish from the public memory. For many citizens, the overwhelming evidence for the whispering road was confirmation of a supernatural presence. Several theological dissertations of the 1970s and 1980s point to the road as evidence of God. However, over the years, the community of believers dwarfed. Perhaps support dissipated because the road was never reported as saying anything novel. If it had stated something outside of our nation's catch phrase lexicon it might have remained in our consciousness.

By 2013, American amnesia was complete. No Internet websites or sources confirm the facts of the whispering road. All quotes and newspaper articles collect dust on limited access microfilm in archives at the Library of Congress, the National Capital Park and Planning Commission, and the state highway departments of Maryland and Virginia. The chill of majority skepticism has silenced witnesses and lead most of them to believe their experiences were imaginary.

It still whispers, though. Listen.

Nathan Blanchard grew up in Montgomery County, Maryland. After living in Nashville for several years, he returned to the DC/Baltimore area in 2009, where he currently lives with his wife.

DC Public Library Book Cart
Photograph by John Muller

POST-COLD WAR
by Herb Guggenheim

Night.

Driving down East-West Highway, we see it—
emanating from behind us,
casting pink white light onto our dashboard, mirrors, and windshield.
It swells to a brightness we've never seen before,
bears down on us like maybe a trucker's fallen asleep—only brighter.

Oh my God! I think
(because I don't have original thoughts at times like this)
It's the end!
Somebody just detonated something bad—
really bad.

And I wonder—
as I've sometimes wondered in the past—
if it *is* something bad,
will it vaporize my brain before signals of pain, loss, and regret
ever have a chance to reach it?
One can only hope.

Then, I wonder if it's the Christian End Time—
The Rapture I think they call it.
Or that gremlin Shatner sees on *The Twilight Zone*. Only
we're not on an airplane
and I'm not Shatner.

As it turns out, it's none of these things.

My wife, who's very observant,

spots sparks showering down from a fast receding phone pole
like the dying trails of some Disney World skyrocket.

A transformer's blown and,
what with all the bends in the road,
we're not sure if any other drivers got the full impact like we did.

Streetlights are out of course.
Houses are dark and we're concentrating on the road
so it doesn't occur to us to fire up our cell phones
and alert the power company that the Rapture's
        starting up so they'd better send some men.
That call will just have to wait.

At least now, I think,
if the end does come,
I'll sort of know what to expect.

Herb Guggenheim received his MA from the Writing Seminars at Johns Hopkins University and his PhD from the Center for Writers at the University of Southern Mississippi. His poems and short stories have appeared in literary magazines including the Beloit Poetry Journal, Gargoyle, and the Florida Review. His book Sunset at the Hotel Mira Mar: New and Selected Poems was published by Infinity in 2011.

AMERICORPS
by Jonathan Hunger

On most afternoons upon coming back from a hard day of working AmeriCorps, I return to our communal couch, plop down, crack open a box of Cheez-Its, eat about a third of it, watch back episodes of *The Daily Show*, and space out. I'm typically zonked, drained, and not really prepared to do much of anything else for the night.

Yes. It's that bad.

Today, however, I feel much more motivated, even inspired. That is because today, July 23, 2004, is my second to last day of work. My yearlong AmeriCorps term of service ends tomorrow and I've had the feeling that I'd better squeeze every last bit of fun out of DC before I head back to New Jersey for a life of suburban melancholy, slogging away through grad school. And that means pushing myself on a weekday to take action.

So, what to do? I wander about the house looking for my five soon-to-be erstwhile team members; none is around, which is unusual, because on most days they are as pooped as I am from doing construction at Habitat for Humanity all day. I'll concede, however, that of the whole group I'm a particularly bad case.

"Juan-yyyyy!"

I hear a cry of my beloved nickname from up above, though it sounds more distant than I expect. I walk to the bottom of the stairs and look up, but no one is there. Then, again I hear the call.

Upon reaching the top of the stairs I check all the bedrooms, but they are empty. Farther down the hall I see a ray of light coming through the ceiling, and there I find an opening to the roof, which I never knew existed. I guess I should've been more intrepid this past year and explored my own house a little bit better.

I pull myself through the opening and come out on the roof where I see Aisha sitting, smoking a cigarette, looking out at the bright blue July sky.

"I never knew we could get to the roof," I say to her. "This is kinda cool."

"Oh, yah, I come up here like once a week."

"You do?"

"Sure, Juany! Can't smoke in the house, and I like to change it up from the porch sometimes, ya know?" She takes a long drag and blows out smoke rings.

Though I build houses as part of my AC gig for Habitat, I don't do so well on roofs. At work they usually keep me on the ground floor, especially after a terrifying incident one day putting up shingles. It actually involved Aisha, before we became friends, but as we are on good terms now, I opt not to reminisce with her about this particular story. But to you, dear reader, I can say: Aisha was in a foul mood on the day that just the two of us worked on the roof together. And, given my fear of heights, all I could think throughout the entire traumatic experience was, "I'm scared…and I hate you!"

Now, atop my own house, I peek out over the edge and look down on the neighborhood below. Fortunately, our home has a flattop, so, unlike when I'm on the angled-roof houses at our worksite, I have less of a chance of rolling off and plummeting to my untimely demise.

I look east down the tree-lined block at the red brick row-houses on Burke Street. I then peer over my shoulder at the armory building and RFK stadium, just a few blocks away. I was only ever at the stadium once, to see the US women's soccer team play. Rumors are swirling that a new baseball team could be playing there soon.

"Hey, Juany, remember that time we did Halloween at the neighbors' place?"

"I missed it."

"You did?" she asks in disbelief. "Why?"

"Guess I was feeling a little shy back then."

"Juany, that's crazy! Did you at least see the decorations they put up all along Burke?"

"Yeah, on my way to the Metro. I walked past them. Almost had a fake ghost fall on me. That was the closest I got to it."

"Oh, bummer, Juany! That's so lame."

"I'll make up for it tomorrow night."

Our big end-of-year bash is at the house on Saturday night. We had invited every other AmeriCorps crew in the DC area, and encouraged them to bring along everyone they knew, too. The night's theme is "Anything for a Dollar." That is to say, if you accept a dollar from anyone at the party, then you must do whatever they want. I'm sure everything will be completely appropriate and PG-rated. I am just curious in what condition we'll leave the house.

I look to the southwest at Massachusetts Avenue where they filmed the Tom Cruise movie Minority Report. It is a block of row houses with a large triangular island in the middle of the street. Early in the movie, Tom bursts into one of the houses to arrest a guy for, presumably, being responsible for a crime he did not yet commit. I liked most of the movie, but not the end, and tell Aisha so.

"Yah, that sucked, man," she says and takes a final drag on her cigarette. She stubs it out and flicks the butt off the roof into the back alley below.

Along that stretch of Mass Ave is a playground that we used to walk past on our way to volunteering at the Boys and Girls Club, which is just up the block. I have mostly fond memories of the volunteering experience; I used to play basketball with the kids at the Club when they were done with school. But one day I wasn't paying attention during a game and got bonked on the head with the ball. It got a big, boisterous laugh from what seemed like the entire Club, so I felt satisfied that I was doing my job effectively.

I notice a man walking his two dainty, foot tall, Cousin Itt-like dogs down 18th Street, which runs alongside our house. Each dog has a ribbon on its head, one red and one blue. I watch the pair approach one of the biggest dogs I've ever seen in my life, which is locked in behind a chain-link fence. The two tiny dogs begin what they clearly think is ferocious, hysterical barking and then, to my surprise, actually leap in the air multiple times trying to hurdle the high fence to get at their new foe. The big dog looks back in puzzlement and responds with a couple of deep cursory barks, but it seems to just be going through the motions; there is no heart in the effort. The owner yanks the two little ones away and they prance off in an apparent victory march.

"Will you write me from Jersey next year?" Aisha asks me abruptly.

"Oh, of course," I say.

"I don't mean email. I want real letters."

"I think I can do that."

"I'm gonna miss this place," she says.

Aisha reaches into her pocket and takes out her cigarette pack. But instead of lighting up another one, she only looks at it and then absentmindedly plays with it in her hands.

"But you're off to New Orleans in a few days," I say. "That should be fun; Mardi Gras and all that jazz."

"Yeah," she says, not really sounding like she is paying attention. "Is Gretchen coming to the party tomorrow?"

"I think she'll be there," I say. Gretchen is my hipster friend with a mysterious past.

"Good! 'Cause I'll miss her, too."

The last time Gretchen visited the house, we couldn't find a corkscrew for our wine, so she took the bottle out to the street and, with a high-pitched maniacal laugh, smashed the neck off on the curb. I worried about one of the poor neighborhood doggies accidentally stepping on the shards of glass; she was unconcerned.

I see two young women walking through the alley below us, which I've sometimes used as a shortcut to the Metro station. One time I didn't use it because my friend Joshua was visiting and he balked at the thought of passing through since he suspected it was too dangerous to do so at night. I was surprised by his reaction; though Joshua is a short mild-mannered intellectual, he had helped in the apprehension of a large and violent rider on the Metro system a few weeks earlier. Personally, I'd pick the alleyway any day.

I hear a sound of shuffling and scratching to our left. We look over and see three neighbors I've never met setting up beach chairs on their roof. They smile and flash a thumbs-up at me, in what I can only assume is an act of hipster irony, and I return the gesture.

A few more minutes go by and I begin to get antsy. My fear of heights isn't helping matters, so I decide to skedaddle. I bid Aisha adieu and make my way back down the ladder into the house, whistling a Drifters song that, for some reason, suddenly pops into my head. I continue my search of the house for life, but find none. Out through the front window, however, I do spot a human head. It is Anne sitting on our couch out on the porch.

"Hey," I say to her as I walk outside. "What's shakin'?"

"Hey, hey, hey, 'Juany'," she replies. Anne says 'Juany' with some derision as she thinks it is a ridiculous and juvenile nickname for me, and often tells me so. The name actually doesn't bother me very much, but I've explained to her before that it's not a name of my choosing, and that these things just stick.

Anne appears to have found a fedora and is wearing it pulled far down on her head, almost over her eyes. I sit down on the cushioned chair situated next to the couch.

"Do you think we'll ever come back here?" she asks me.

"To this house?"

"To DC."

"I think so," I say.

"Would you live here?"

"I don't know."

We sit in silence for a few minutes looking out on Burke Street. A couple of the neighborhood kids are riding their scooters on the sidewalk. Gary, the friendly alley cat, looks up our porch stairs and meows, which I assume translates roughly to "hello" or "feed me" or "pay attention to me." A small group of teenage boys has a basketball with them and is presumably headed for the courts at the elementary school up on D Street. The courts sit across from the small neighborhood computer center; it brings back memories of when I used to feverishly check my email there whenever I could, waiting to hear back from potential grad programs for next year.

"I think I might travel the world," says Anne, breaking the silence.

"I think I might travel New Jersey," I reply.

She gives me a pitying smile.

"Feeling cynical?" she asks.

"No. I shouldn't say that. It'll be fine."

"You can come visit me at my first stop in Central America. I hear they have Habitat there, too," she says.

"Maybe," I reply. "But I'm afraid it might break my streak of days working Habitat uninjured. Don't want to push my luck. Know what I mean?"

"Chicken."

"We'll see," I say. "You got hurt, like, three times this year. Shouldn't you be more sympathetic?"

Anne stands up.

"I'll let you think it over," she says, and then disappears into the house.

I switch over from the chair to the couch so I can lie down. I look up at the ceiling over the porch and close my eyes, imagining the party tomorrow night. I turn my head and look out at the street.

I hop down the stoop and make my way down Burke. I feel like an adventure.

Jonathan Hunger joined AmeriCorps after graduating from the University of Maryland, and presently works as a high school History and Special Education teacher in Bethesda, Maryland. He lives with his wife in Virginia.

THE OLDER MAN
by Lauren Yaffe

T.O.M. was a Comedian, capital C—*always*. If I asked a simple, "How are you?" he would launch into one of numerous accents. British: "Jolly well spiffy today, what?" Ersatz Indian: "I am quite cosmic today, sahib!" Or hippie: "Groovin'." He'd follow with a maniacal laugh which made me feel small for asking such a routine question, overly sensitive for feeling small, and inanely jocular. Some commented, "He's always *on*, isn't he?" I liked this staginess in Tom, thinking it showed wit and charisma, qualities I strove to emulate.

Of the clubs Tom performed at in the Washington area, the most regular haunt was DC Space, a now-defunct playhouse/biker bar on E Street. We'd enter through the back door as the bouncer looked on: Tom, his comedy troupe, and me, panting under a crate of equipment. Sometimes, if the regular techie didn't show, I'd run lights and sound, exchanging a secret glance with Tom as I cued up the tape player for the next skit. Mostly, though, I was his groupie. Watching him on stage, I felt electrified: my boyfriend, the comedian!

During intermission, there was free beer for the troupe, me included. No one thought to card me. Once the manager unloaded his girlfriend woes on me, adding, "Hey, if I break up with her, you wanna go out with me?"

"You're too old for me," I teased.

"No!" he pleaded, "I'm only 24." Exactly Tom's age.

After the show, Tom and I would take a walk along the downtown sidewalk, littered with broken glass and trash, drained bottles of Thunderbird. I felt as if I'd clicked my ruby slippers and been dropped down in Oz. The night shimmered with forbidden lateness; shards of glass announced not the shoddiness of the neighborhood but my daring to venture there. And, as Tom took my hand, the graffiti blared how fortunate I was to be loved, noticed even, by this man.

Tom asked, in an exaggerated Southern drawl, "Did we do ahlraht?"

"They loved you," I cooed.

Then he asked about a new skit. I consistently misconstrued questions from adults, assuming they wanted the truth and that I was able to provide it. Tom spoke admiringly of firecracker women he'd dated who wouldn't let him pull punches, examples for me to live up to. But no one had shown me how to do this--certainly not my mother who let my father ride roughshod over her during their 25 years of marriage. Nor my father, more absent than present in my life since long before their divorce. "The skit was a bit long," I tried, "and too hammy."

"Aren't we the brilliant critic!" he snapped. "Look who thinks she knows something about comedy?" He stormed ahead. Moments later, he turned, his powerful gaze on me now warm. Everything was fine.

We spent nights at the Georgetown rowhouse Tom shared with friends or crept up to my own bedroom—behavior my mother willfully ignored. In the morning, Tom drove to his day job. I rode a yellow bus to Bethesda-Chevy Chase High School, which though I lived in DC, my father's Maryland address qualified me to attend. I swallowed No-Doz in first period and during lunch when I did my homework. After school, I scooped ice cream at Baskin-Robbins to save for college.

Before Tom, my girlfriends and I would roam the streets and alleys of my Chevy Chase neighborhood, the macadam quilting our footfalls. Walking meant freedom. Wherever our feet took us was territory claimed: porched houses and thick oak trees defending them, parked station wagons, a bicycle on its side by the curb, honeysuckle boughs draped over garage doors, morning glory vines fingering through fence slats. We peered in windows at families huddled over dinner tables, and televisions flashing a sad blue while we hoped, always, to find a more exciting scene—a fight, perhaps, or someone undressing.

Our conversations pulsed with more excitement than any scene witnessed in a window. We traversed untrod paths of thought and language. One of us would make up a word: *coumanta*, for instance, then another define it: the exact angle and color of a sun ray hitting a Japanese maple leaf in winter at dawn. We strove to notice life's every nuance. We were learning about hanging out and friendship, about the slow surrealism of marijuana, and how music can swirl around you and define an experience. How relaxed that time was, with no agenda but to do well enough to get into college.

Enter Tom. Mapping *his* mind quickly replaced meandering walks. I forgot about conversation, threading words into glorious webs. Romance, I decided, far outstripped friendship. I gloried in Tom. No matter how unimportant I felt myself to be (an idea Tom frequently reinforced), I knew that, through him, I had access to something important: adulthood.

Adulthood shined with ordinariness. It was thrillingly blasé. Staying out dancing all night, having sex with my boyfriend weren't earthshaking experiences, nothing to giggle about in the back of algebra class. They were meaningful, yes, but meaningful in the sense of living out my life, *not* needing to brag about how little sleep I'd gotten, or how drunk, what "base" I'd gone to. That my friends found these cause for giggles distanced me further from them and their world.

Tom introduced me to a bounty of earthly delights: artsy walks along the canal, Ethiopian restaurants in Adams Morgan with food spicier than I could bear, cozy beer pubs with exotic bottles lining their brick walls. We went rock climbing. We skinny-dipped in a private lagoon. We drove to New York City and met managers of the "big" clubs (whom Tom said I charmed with my simple black dress and quick smile). Tom was capable, worldly, funny. By my association with him I would become those things as well. When he and his friends spouted poetry and politics, I tried to look silently wise. I knew nothing of politics, didn't care to know, but I was horrified to think someone might catch me acting my age.

My age. I went to great lengths to disguise it. First, I ditched my friends. I found it impossible to convey the sophistication of my relationship with Tom to my teenaged friends, with their puerile worries about whether to keep to backseat petting or "go all the way." Most nights, Tom slept beside me. He practically lived at my house. I had bypassed the stage of giddy outdoor romance. If I had plans with girl friends and then Tom asked me out, I'd cancel with the girl friends. Eventually, I dismissed them altogether.

The second thing I did was go mum. Tom was a counselor in the youth group to which I belonged. Though he and I never discussed this substantial breach of ethics, when we went to meetings, he'd drop me off a block away so we would arrive separately. When the group discussed relationships, I said nothing of my experiences. I reasoned that I didn't need to brag. Later I realized it is not bragging to say that your boyfriend is swallowing you whole. But *then* I wouldn't let on that I was in over my head, that a part of me ached for the easy comfort of my friends and our slow walks. *Look how much I'm learning!* I told myself.

I learned how to listen to adults and ask questions about their lives, to make them feel important. I learned to joke when I felt low, to sit unobtrusively while Tom wrote important skits. I learned to pretend to climax when he did, so he would sleep victorious. I was too proud of having a sexual life to examine whether or not it was satisfying.

I learned abandonment. Once, at a party at Tom's house, he slipped out with another woman. Not having a ride home, I spent the night in his bed, shaking mercilessly, ashamed to face Tom's housemates. I learned to share Tom with the women he seduced and listen supportively when he talked of them since I was, as he reminded me, his secret, *special* love. If I felt hurt, it was only the weakness and insecurity of youth. I learned to seduce other men and hurt them too. I was a good study.

Once Tom asked me along to dinner with him and a former girlfriend, someone he'd almost married. I felt glum and awkward, at a loss to keep up conversation. I asked how she liked her job. "Don't make small talk," Tom chided. "Be *interesting*!" I felt monstrously plain. The price of having a capable, worldly, funny boyfriend: I had to be those things as well.

I spent two of my most formative years, from 15 to 17, with Tom before finally escaping to the world of college and *real* adulthood. Before that, I tried several times to break off with him, suggesting we be "just friends", but he always lured me back with the assurance that he loved me, that we were special. Which now I see, we *were*. Special because he, as no high school boy could, introduced me to the entanglements and complexities of relationships. Because he showed me the determination and the details necessary to pursue an artistic career; because he had an infectious energy and drive to experience the world with all senses; and he included me in the experience. I could have, and would have, learned all this on my own in time but that was not the education I craved. I was not interested in a gradual coming of age, a lover as in the dark as I was, groping for light beside me. I wanted a bullet of knowledge that bleeds and sears as it passes through, emblazoning scars that toughen over time. The gravest sacrifice I made for that quick, burning knowledge: my friendships with women, our walks and ambling conversations. Eventually, I had to double back to recover what I could of those, and painstakingly learn a moral and caring way to treat myself and others. I'm now wary of people who are always "on." I know that energy, and don't need to be near it or learn from it anymore. But I understand why that 15-year-old girl did.

Lauren Yaffe *holds an MFA from Warren Wilson College. Her stories, poems and essays have appeared in* Alaska Quarterly, Cottonwood Review, Calliope, Frigate, English Journal, Fiction Weekly, Willow Review, Ellipsis, Voices from the Spectrum, Altered States Anthology, *and others. She lives in Brooklyn with her husband, children, dogs, turtle and some 20,000 red wriggler worms.*